LONG BEFORE COLUMBUS
How the Ancients Discovered America

LONG BEFORE COLUMBUS

HOW THE ANCIENTS DISCOVERED AMERICA

HANS HOLZER

INTRODUCED BY
BARBARA HAND CLOW

BEAR & COMPANY
PUBLISHING
SANTA FE, NEW MEXICO

LIBRARY OF CONGRESS CATALOGING-IN-PUBLICATION DATA

Holzer, Hans
    Long before Columbus / how the ancients discovered America / by
Hans Holzer ; foreword by Barbara Hand Clow.
        p.   cm.
    Includes bibliographical references.
    ISBN 0-939680-86-6
    1. America—Discovery and exploration—Pre-Columbian. 2. Megalithic
monuments—New Hampshire. 3. New Hampshire—Antiquities. I. Title.
E103.H83 1992
970.01′1—dc20   91-40844
                                                                        CIP

Text, interior photographs, and illustrations © 1992 by Hans Holzer
Foreword © 1992 by Barbara Hand Clow

Bear & Company, Inc.
Santa Fe, NM 87504-2860

Front cover photograph: Bob Longacre © 1992

Back cover photograph: Richard Erdoes © 1992

Cover & interior design: Chris Kain

Author photo: Peter Lehner

Editing: Gail Vivino

Typography: Buffalo Publications

PHOTO CREDITS: Hans Holzer: 1, 2, 6, 7, 8, 9, 10, 15, 21, 22, 23, 24, 25, 26, 27,
29, 34. Osborn Stone: 3, 4, 5, 11, 12, 13, 14, 16, 17, 18, 19, 20, 28, 30, 31, 32. Robert
Stone: 33.

Printed in the United States of America by R.R. Donnelley

9 8 7 6 5 4 3 2 1

To those who believe in
this research and these conclusions

CONTENTS

ILLUSTRATIONS

MAPS

Two gatefold maps:

FOREWORD

When Professor Hans Holzer asked me to introduce *Long Before Columbus*, I asked him, "Why me?" since as acquisitions editor at Bear & Company, I do not introduce books unless my own research is directly related to the subject being discussed. In this case, Dr. Holzer felt deep resonance with my continuing study of the profound effects on human consciousness of the eruption of Santorini, or Thera, almost four thousand years ago as described in my *Mind Chronicles* trilogy. This eruption set off the wanderings of the "Sea Peoples," the Mediterranean clans who sailed the world from about 1500 B.C. to 1100 B.C. When I read *Long Before Columbus*, it seemed very likely to me that the original builders of "America's Stonehenge" were some of these Sea Peoples: this great cataclysm might have brought people all the way to the shores of North America! Many respected scholars have also stressed the critical impact on ancient history of this eruption in the cradle of civilization—the Aegean—and the possibility of influences all the way across the Atlantic is fascinating.

I agreed to do the foreword, but it wasn't until visiting Mystery Hill in September 1991 that I realized the deeper levels of importance of this site for the collective unconscious of North Americans. As many of us are now beginning to realize, the true story of our ancient heritage has been systematically suppressed in our literature, formal education, and family backgrounds. In the pivotal year of 1992, when we are being asked to celebrate the "discovery of America" by Columbus, this megalithic site, which scientific evidence reveals was built 3,500 years ago, is a major challenge to the official story of our past.

The facts are that in literature freely exploring archaeological remains in North America—books that are dismissed as being "fantastic" or not sufficiently scholarly by the old-paradigm scholars—it is very obvious that Celts, Sea Peoples, Hebrews, Africans, and many other groups have visited and/or settled in North America during the last four thousand years and probably earlier. If the reader wishes to explore these questions, read Barry Fell's *America B.C.*, William McGlone and Philip Leonard's *Ancient Celtic America*, Olson Tryggvi's *Early Voyages and Northern Ap-*

proaches, 1000-1632, Trento Salvatore's *The Search for Lost America,* Alexander von Wuthenau's *Unexpected Faces in Ancient America,* or *Manitou: The Sacred Landscapes of New England's Native Civilization,* to name the most well-known sources. You will see that the story about North American heritage that has been put forth in traditional schools and in official sources is a blatant fabrication. Who is there left who really believes that Christopher Columbus "discovered" America in 1492? So, why do we allow this to remain as "our story?" Remember, our story is our own creative matrix from which we view our current reality. The tale of our past that we believe is accurate describes our ancestors and is the basis of how we think our land has been occupied. This "past" then influences our actions in the present moment.

This fabrication about our origins has been a vehicle used too long to keep us in the dark about our past, our roots, and the original people of our country—America, "the land of the free and the brave." How can we be free and brave if our identity is founded on a lie? How many of us were told in grade school that we were lucky to be born free, white, and heterosexual in America? The term "America" itself is chauvinistic, since it leaves out Central and South America, as if the United States is all there is of the Western Hemisphere. But, you may ask, why harp on this? Because this fabrication is what continues to perpetuate the colonialism that resulted in the genocide of indigenous people, who are the true carriers of the story of the land for all peoples.

The genocide resulting from Christopher Columbus's "discovery" of America, along with the "civilizing" of Mexico by Cortés, resulted in the murder of around eighty million indigenous people beginning in the sixteenth century. This behavior continues wherever indigenous tribal people still exist in jungles and forests, and economic expansion threatens their way of life. In fact, current Judeo-Christian colonialism is fueling the very destruction of the Earth itself. This economic expansion and colonialism are based on the Judeo-Christian theological doctrine of "dominion" over the Earth, and the result has always been systematic rape of the planet.

This violence will continue until we refuse to put up with the prevailing lie. That is why the struggle for recognition of truth in 1992 is so important. Just when we seem to be helpless in the face of huge forces bent on destruction, a creative idea has emerged that has the power to shadow dance us beyond these forces. We are in the midst of a big choice during

1992: are we going to continue to accede to these lies, or are we going to reclaim the power lurking deep inside *our true story?*

What do I mean? It is exciting that ancient peoples from all over the world graced our land with their spirits and temples. It is exciting that the indigenous people of the Americas may be our very own ancestors, considering all the ancient travels back and forth across seas. It is exciting that a great and complete megalithic solar and lunar calendar is located in North Salem, New Hampshire. If we are to terminate the lie—"Columbus sailed the ocean blue and discovered America in 1492"—we must replace it with a new story, and that is why Dr. Holzer's book is so important. Besides Mystery Hill itself, there are hundreds of other megalithic stone sites in North America. Mystery Hill is the tip of an iceberg.

I find it truly odd that a site scientifically carbon-dated and bristlecone-pine verified to 1525 B.C. in the United States is not well known. As it turns out, there is reason for such an extensive cover-up. This site proves, beyond a shadow of doubt, that the ancient people who erected it—whether they are indigenous, as brilliantly researched by James Mavor and Byron Dix in *Manitou*, or whether they are a mix of seafaring races—were a people of great mathematical and astronomical sophistication.

I am an archaeoastronomer and an astrologer—seeker of understanding about Earth by means of studying sky patterns. I have traveled the world in search of megalithic stone temples and astronomical devices that once instructed humankind in the science of Earth/sky harmony. In this age lost to materialism, which has resulted in disconnected spirituality, I've been involved in a search to recover the ancient Earth library of synchronicity and harmony that exists within megalithic technology. I have chosen to discover the ancient knowledge in hopes it will yield survival keys that I know we will soon require.

When I began my ascent to the top of Mystery Hill during the fall of 1991, I knew I would be exploring an ancient repository of megalithic records of critical importance. But I had a couple of major concerns. First of all, I had been especially concerned about the methodology used to substantiate the material in *Long Before Columbus*, which includes a very careful explanation of the site's archaeological records combined with various techniques for psychic and intuitive exploration of the location.

However, since the importance of this site has been systematically ignored by academic archaeologists, I decided that Dr. Holzer had every right to explore it as he wished.

I was even more concerned that the research for this manuscript was largely undertaken in the 1970s, though it had been slightly updated. However, I felt the importance of the material outweighed this problem—were we to have another generation pass by who would not know that North America has a very ancient heritage? Much to my delight, when I visited Mystery Hill, I verified for myself Dr. Holzer's claim that no new significant research has been yet published on this ancient site, one of the most important in the world. The reason for this is obvious: this site will not be taken seriously as long as the United States is determined to deify Columbus in order to protect its colonialistic worldview. Thus, the publication of this book in the five-hundredth anniversary of Columbus is most significant.

It is my hope that *Long Before Columbus*, along with efforts by others concerned about such sites, will finally force academic archaeologists to study prehistoric North America seriously. Since America's Stonehenge has been scientifically carbon-dated and bristlecone-pine verified to 1525 B.C., it holds great power to force a massive revision of North American history. And, I might add, the scene in the United States is not totally bleak. In the summer of 1991, I visited Cahokia, the site of a major Mound Builder city just east of St. Louis that now has a marvelous and enlighted visitor center. The Mound Builders were a prehistoric culture in North America that built extensive earthworks from 1500 B.C. to A.D. 1000. This site is now considered to be of international importance and is protected by the United Nations. I hope this will be the case with "America's Stonehenge" in the near future. If Mystery Hill had been located in Europe, it would have been afforded such respect a hundred years ago.

It is likely that this round stone outcropping high above the Merrimack River was treeless when it was used as a solar and lunar calculator. As you will see from the site maps and photographs, beyond the central site there lies a great circle of standing stones that mark the equinoxes, solstices, North Star, and, I suspect, lunar nodes. Since trees had gradually obscured the alignments to the standing stones (some of which fell down over time) and the main interest in the site in the eighteenth and nineteenth centuries was to quarry the central site for local roads and buildings, the outer astronomical circle was ignored and is now basically complete after some restoration twenty years ago.

Fortunately, the key stones were either still standing or were still lying on the ground when excavation began in the 1970s. To assist in seeing the importance of this fact, a comparison to the great megalithic calculator of Avebury Circle in Wilshire, England, can be used. There, so many stones were carted away or broken up by fanatical Christians that it is now very difficult to ascertain its original scientific astronomical alignments. However, the New England Antiquities Research Association (NEARA) has been thankfully protecting and researching the Mystery Hill site, and while I was there, I got to watch them carefully raising another marker stone. This circular calculator is an ancient megalithic library of astronomical research because it is so complete. As many readers may know, there is much wonderful exploration of this science—archaeoastronomy—being done at this time. As one of the many researchers, I would like to contribute my own small discoveries at Mystery Hill, since the things I found myself back up Dr. Holzer's belief that its builders must have been Minoan seafarers.

In 1964, Robert Stone, who has owned and protected Mystery Hill for many years, began to suspect that the large stones in the walls circling the main site had an astronomical function. In order to decode an astronomical calculator, it is necessary to locate the central point of all the alignments in order to observe solar, lunar, or stellar bodies rising behind the standing stones from the central point. Since the Sacrificial Table was obviously of such major importance in the central site, Stone first attempted to view from the alignments from that table.

By cutting some swathes through the trees to a few standing stones, he discovered that the central point of alignments was actually thirty feet directly to the north of the Sacrificial Table. This point is on a great round rock where there is now a very helpful viewing station constructed by NEARA. Stone discovered that it aligns with a standing stone to the north over which rises the North Celestial Pole Star—now Polaris, but it would have been Thuban in 1525 B.C.

A pathway through key fixed stars around the central axis of the Earth traces the twenty-six-thousand-year equinox-precession cycle, and this is the function of the standing stone that marks the North Pole Star.

However, I believe that something else of great significance has not yet been noticed: an alignment to the central point from the south. This alignment is established by a very unusual standing triangular stone just a few inches from the north edge of the Sacrificial Table, visible in photo 8. I will refer to this as the North Sacrifical Table Standing Stone (NSTSS). For some reason, no published research that I know of has taken particular note of this large stone.

Astronomically, the alignment from the Sacrificial Table over the tip of the NSTSS to the central alignment point (which once might have been marked by a wooden or stone pole or staff) and north to the North Standing Stone connects the central alignment point to the Sacrifical Table. This further establishes that the builders of the astronomical calculator understood the equinox precession cycle, which would greatly increase respect for the intelligence of these ancient people.

The 1525 B.C. carbon dating of the site described in detail by Dr. Holzer was accomplished in the central site. If a similar carbon dating could be accomplished in the organic layer directly below the outer stones when they were originally raised, we would then know the date of when these ancient builders created this calculator, thus proving that they knew of the sophisticated equinox precession cycle. There is little doubt that the whole central site is megalithic, considering the style of its construction and the carbon-dating results, and it is likely that the astronomical calculator is megalithic as well, since a similar type of astronomical devices exist all over the world from megalithic cultures, built mostly before 1500 B.C.

It is also possible that the central site was considered to be very powerful energetically by later people, and the surrounding calculator might have been constructed after the central site. I find Mavor and Dix's *Manitou* to be a very significant contribution in the field of archaeo-astronomy, and due to the shape of the standing stones in the calculator, they are almost all "Manitou stones," stones that held great power for Native Americans. Mavor and Dix argue that most of the ancient stone remains in new England are the technology of indigenous North Americans. I mention this because I see a wonderful "both/and" of thousands of years of cross-cultural exchange across the seas. It is exciting to think of the ancestors of the Algonquins honoring the geomantic power of Mystery Hill by building a great solar, lunar, and stellar calculator to teach astronomy to "visitors." However, we will not know anything more about these questions until the calculator is scientifically carbon dated and the results published. Meanwhile, the NSTSS is of critical importance regarding the interfacing between the central site and the calculator.

The alignment to the NSTSS from the North Pole Star would seem to indicate concurrent construction of the central site and the outer circle of stones. It also points to the possibility that whatever went on with the Sacrificial Table and its connection to the "speaking tube" below (described by Dr. Holzer in the text) is related to issues of the Great Ages, the 2,160-year long cycles that comprise the precession of the equinoxes. For any student of ancient cosmology, this possibility is of extreme importance.

To lessen readers' possible concerns about human sacrifice, I interject here that I think it is extremely unlikely that this is at issue. First of all, the Sacificial Table is the perfect size for the sacrifice of bulls rather than humans, and if Dr. Holzer is correct in his belief that the 1525 B.C. builders were probably Minoan seafarers, it is highly likely that the sacrifices were of oxen and bulls. An archaeological search for bull remains would be of great help in this regard. It is also possible that the running-ibex inscription within the central chamber indicates sacrifice of lambs, deer, or ibex. However, as one who has recently attended water buffalo sacrifices in Tana Toraja in Indonesia, I would suggest that we must reserve judgmental tendencies about ancient rituals. It is very hard to enter into the mind-set of the ancients, and negativity blocks insight.

Keeping in mind the alignment of the Sacrificial Table to the North Star, we can see that it is likely that propitiation here to the gods and goddesses through sacrifice is related to the cycles of the Great Ages. To put it simply, this would mean that the prayers and rituals of these people were connected to the symbols of the Great Ages: the great bull during the Age of Taurus, from 4400 to 2200 B.C., and the warrior during the Age of Aries, from 2200 B.C. to A.D. 0. The ibex or running horned animal in the chamber is another typical symbol for the Age of Aries, which was the prevailing cycle when the Oracle Chamber was built. The ancient symbology of the zodiac in the sky is ultimately animal totemic, and as consciousness emerges in time, the totemic importance of the Great Ages and their association with animal archetypes yields key insights into the ancient mind. Mystery Hill would seem to be a major source of information in this area. Since Mavor and Dix's brilliant research on another astronomical calculator site called "Calendar One" has yielded data indicating usage over at least twelve thousand years, there is good reason to investigate ritual association to the Great Ages.

I encourage readers to delve into this fascinating research. I bring these issues up because they present the possibility that the origin of Mystery Hill goes much further back in time than even 1525 B.C.; it is possible that the builders Dr. Holzer cites were working with a power site that was already thousands of years old!

It is because of these possibilities that I applaud his very free-form and entertaining investigation showing that some psychics felt extreme antiquity at Mystery Hill. Since academic archaeologists have declined a scientific investigation of the site at this time, the work of psychics is needed. On that note, I too am a psychic, and my "read" was that Mystery Hill was found to be a power vortex from Earth to sky twenty-five thousand years ago. The glacial recession in the area would have removed any physical traces before 10,000 B.C.

While touring the site, I took note of the alignment from the NSTSS, then I stood above the outdoor courtyard (was it always outdoors?) of the Sacrificial Table for a few hours contemplating the table and the NSTSS. Due to the importance of the table, I was surprised that the 1991 guide material as well as other published materials on this site that I had seen did not call attention to the NSTSS.

Next, what stood out for me were very prominent and beautiful natural inverted "V" markings on the south face of the NSTSS. The worked inscription of the inverted V is very common and important at Mystery Hill, and it is a visual clue that marks alignments and location of Earth energy. This type of inscription is related to the Goddess, according to goddess researcher and archaeologist Marija Gimbutas, and the natural inverted V's on the NSTSS south face could be seen twenty feet away where I stood. Megalithic people highly revered stones and crystals that contained significant natural marks, and these marks on the NSTSS, combined with its placement right on the north edge of the Sacrificial Table, revealed its great importance to me. I suspect this to be verified by continuing research.

My second discovery concerns an ancient chamber called the "Watch House," which is situated on the hill approaching the main site. The guide leaflet points out that this structure might have been a chamber for a guard and states that "nothing of significance" has been found here. This type of remark always tells me exactly where to go, and so I crawled into the little chamber, which opens to the south and was fairly well lighted by the fall sunlight.

I discovered that directly in the back wall of the chamber is a very significant gray granite stone with white-quartz protrusions in it that form the double eye revered by the Cretan goddess culture. This finding supports Dr. Holzer's theory that Minoans built the central site, as their culture was the last culture of the Goddess. Around the two white-quartz crystal eyes—the left eye larger than the right one—is a natural, very red ferrous deposit that outlines the eyes, making the rock very beautiful. This rock would have been highly revered by all megalithic people, as it would be highly revered by Native Americans now. Any thought that this stone placement is accidental is absurd, because it is located in the place of maximum light in the back wall facing the entrance; it is a marker of the Eye Goddess.

To know more about this chamber astronomically would require additional visits to the site, but I believe that this double eye is intended to indicate to the visitor that the Eye Goddess is guardian of Mystery Hill. This likelihood is further supported by the fact that the 1961 Upper Well excavations yielded large numbers of quartz-crystal clusters that were growing in natural joints or faults in the bedrock, as Dr. Holzer mentions. It is clear that quartz crystals were sacred to the original people here. They were sacred to the Minoans, as they are to Native Americans, and it is possible that this entire complex might have been originally located on Mystery Hill due to the presence of crystals. At the very least, the natural quartz Eye Goddess stone located at the entrance is of major importance, since most megalithic sites have deep connections to the worship of the Great Mother; this is especially true of a site like Mystery Hill, which is a calculator that relates the Earth to the sky.

There is something still deeper that nags me about this site. Dr. Holzer notes that anthropologist Sharon McKern took an interest in colonial inhabitants' knowledge about Mystery Hill since it was such a huge and prominent complex. (In *Manitou*, Mavor and Dix discuss the strong likelihood that these major stone sites were known to the colonial settlers.) McKern suggested that Mystery Hill might have been a site for occult practices in colonial times by underground survivors of the Salem witch cult. Salem Village, where the 1692 trials occurred, extended to Andover, and South Salem, New Hampshire, extended close to North Andover. They are so geographically close that a link is very likely. Salem is a short form of "Jerusalem," and this area most likely carried this name because it was a power place to find links from Earth to heaven.

The witch trials were about possession, and Mystery Hill evokes much about this Judeo-Christian fear complex. In *Beyond Geography: The Western Spirit Against the Wilderness*, a brilliant study of colonial mentality at the time North America was settled, author Frederick Turner equates the Christian fear of possession with fear of wild peoples and of nature. It is this fear that generates the classic Judeo-Christian dominion complex that now threatens the planet with destruction. This complex was first born in Hebrew culture, which claims that the Jews were given dominion over the Earth by Yahweh if they would be faithful to "him." It cannot be an accident that the witch trials of 1692 were in Salem, Massachusetts, and the suppression of the ancient history of Mystery Hill is in nearby Salem, New Hampshire.

Salem, this New Jerusalem, is a place of great power for relearning the ancient arts of synchronization with Gaia by means of praying for the planet at solstices, equinoxes, and other significant stellar points in time. Perhaps there was a cult of seekers of ancient Earth wisdom who were being instructed by the Native elders of the tribes, just as many seek wisdom about the Earth from Native Americans today. The years of 1640 to 1690 were the time of genocide for indigenous people of New England, which culminated in the witch trials of 1692—at that time the two hundredth anniversary of Columbus's "discovery" of America.

Therefore, 1992 is both the five hundredth anniversary of Columbus's visit and the three hundredth anniversary of the Salem witch trials. From my point of view, it is critical for our very survival that we wake up and see that the wilderness of Earth is not a possession and that nobody "discovered" America. She was and always will be a beautiful land of great power and fruition. She needs no man to dominate and control her, and the death of civilization and not nature will prove that. She needs only to breathe and birth in the midst of the movements of the bodies in the sky. Sites like Mystery Hill lie waiting to teach us all about her cycles and ways of expression.

Barbara Hand Clow
Santa Fe, New Mexico
November 1991

Barbara Hand Clow is the author of a trilogy on sacred sites: Eye of the Centaur: A Visionary Guide into Past Lives; Heart of the Christos: Starseeding from the Pleiades, *and* Signet of Atlantis: War in Heaven Bypass.

INTRODUCTION

The vast majority of Americans have never heard of Mystery Hill, except perhaps those living in its immediate vicinity. Yet, in using the popular designation "America's Stonehenge," I am not exaggerating the importance of this ancient site. If it were properly excavated (not partially, as it is now) and if the background of this extraordinary building and hilltop settlement were brought to the attention of people from all walks of life, Mystery Hill would receive an influx of tourists that would be beyond belief, perhaps even beyond what would be desirable. (One shudders to think of washrooms built into some of the lesser ruins, of subterranean passages to divert modern traffic, and of the inevitable graffiti scribbled onto the stones by tourists without any sense of either destiny or manners.)

However, Mystery Hill should remain a mystery no longer, for the evidence clearly shows it to be a major monument erected by ancient European people who traveled to North American shores by ship. Today, the hill is surrounded by trees, but this may not have been the case in antiquity. Named Mystery Hill by Robert Stone, whose family has owned the site since 1958, it is a complex of ruins near North Salem, New Hampshire, about an hour's ride from Boston. What makes it outstanding as an attraction is its European derivation, of course, and the controversy that has up to now surrounded its origin.

Without the approval of "establishment" archaeologists, historians, and official research organizations, Mystery Hill has not been given the serious attention it deserves from both the public and the scholarly community. In a way, this could be compared to the power held by the American Medical Association over what are considered proper treatment methods, proper medicines, and proper theories concerning disease. Any doctor who prescribes treatment beyond what is "officially" sanctioned will often be shunned by his or her colleagues, if not actively persecuted. There seems to be a psychological barrier against anything straying from the norm—the unconscious desire to belong, to conform, to be accepted is so very strong.

One would expect archaeology to be free from such restrictions, deal-

ing, as it does, with tangible materials. Unfortunately, however, the interpretation of these tangible materials is not left entirely to the discre-
tion of trained professionals. References to published opinions concerning
archaeological material are held in high esteem, even if some of the references are merely perpetuating earlier errors. I remember vividly how,
in my own training as an archaeologist, the restraints put upon me made
me restless and doubtful about what I was being taught at the university. For example, I had serious doubts concerning the dating of prehistoric
periods. I had an even more serious problem accepting the notion that
the human race has been civilized for only a very short period in the
planet's history—that we were cavepeople some hundred thousand years
ago and that there was absolutely nothing civilized before that.

As the years went by and I became more familiar with the evidence
for the existence of high civilizations prior to the caveman era, I found
myself in an increasingly negative position with respect to traditional
archaeology. Though my formative years in the field were spent in the
study of what was safe and established, I also had a persistent desire to
ferret out new information, to publish such new information, and thus
to contribute to the knowledge of humanity's past.

I did this with increasing frequency, primarily in the field of ancient
numismatics, a branch of ancient archaeology I embraced at an early stage
in my career. However, my drive to uncover hitherto unknown evidence
from the past became almost an obsession. Simply reporting known facts
no longer interested me. If I could not add some significant new detail
or change previously held opinions through the presentation of new
evidence, my enthusiasm would wane.

Fortunately for my self-esteem, nearly every new theory I proposed
in the professional journals turned out to be exactly what I hoped it would
be, namely, a new discovery. If some of these new discoveries were of only
minor or moderate significance, it did not matter to me. I was glad to
have discovered things that no one else had pointed out before.

Among my additions to archaeological knowledge were: a descrip-
tion of private graffiti on Roman gold coins of the early Christian era
that disclosed some new and very human details about the quasi-religious
thinking of the era; the discovery of secret letters carved into the hair curls
of a Grecian king on a coin from Asia Minor, on which was also inscribed
the name of the native die engraver; the disclosure of little-known facts

concerning a Danubian metropolis called Carnuntum, a city whose history I had written about many years ago; and finally, in a culmination of fifteen years of research, a best-selling book entitled *Star in the East* on the identity of the so-called three kings of the Christmas legend.

As a young student, I was privileged to acquaint myself with the excavations along the Danube River in the area of Carnuntum. Later, traveling extensively, I visited many of the major archaeological sites of Europe, including those in Italy and Greece. Therefore, when I first became acquainted with Mystery Hill, I recognized at once that I was faced with something extraordinary, something that did not quite fit into the landscape. From the start my curiosity was aroused, and I spent many years looking into "the mystery of Mystery Hill," acquainting myself with all the investigative work that had been done until my appearance on the scene. With the help of the indefatigable Robert Stone, I kept abreast of the views expressed by others as well as the progress of excavations.

I refer to Mystery Hill as America's Stonehenge not because it looks similar to that venerable British ruin, but because it may have occupied a similarly dominant position in New England to that occupied by Stonehenge in the southeast of England. One day, when Mystery Hill is a mystery no more and is fully unearthed, my comparison may be taken up by others, but for the present, suffice it to say that Mystery Hill represents one of the great unsolved puzzles on the North American continent. To the orthodox establishment among archaeologists, Mystery Hill is a name to be avoided, and no official investigation is likely to be made of it. This is also true for any archaeological site in the United States that threatens the established order by clearly indicating a presence in the continental United States of visitors from the Old World long before the arrival of Columbus.

In recent years, some reluctant lip service has been paid by the archaeological establishment to the notion that Vikings may have come here before Columbus, but this admission is immediately played down with a remark that the Viking settlements were minor, peripheral, and transitory. However, it is nowadays assumed that Norwegians came to America before Columbus, and the Sons of Norway celebrate this fact with justified pride even if the Sons of Italy continue to honor their Columbus. But to say that travelers in antiquity came to these shores centuries before the Norsemen is indeed heresy, and heresy of the worst kind. When this heresy is accompanied by reasonable evidence suggesting that it happens to be the truth, the need for a reappraisal of our archaeological view of the United States becomes an urgent one—one that can no longer be postponed.

Only recently have respected scholars come forward to establish the truth about this unique monument called Mystery Hill. In his brilliant book *America B.C.*, Professor Barry Fell, epigrapher of the Harvard University marine biology department and one of America's top experts in ancient writings, describes the strangers from afar as Celto-Iberian and Phoenician in origin. In ancient times, Spain and Portugal had a large number of Phoenician settlements alongside the "native" Celtiberian towns. The Phoenicians were both "mainland" Phoenicians from Asia Minor and "colonials" from Carthage—that is, Punic people. Fell believes that Mystery Hill was settled by the ancient Iberian mariners from Portugal, travelers seeking new shipping lanes and chancing upon a landfall on the New England coast.

However, as I will point out in more detail after exploring the evidence in stone, the same people who inhabited Phoenicia in early times also conquered Crete and became known as Minoans. Thus, when I speak of Minoans and Phoenicians, and Fell speaks of Celtiberians and Phoenicians, we are talking about people of the same period, with one exception—that of point of origin. Fell traces his material mainly back to Portugal and Spain, while I go beyond these points of departure to the original homelands of the travelers, that is, to Crete and Phoenicia. The strangers traveled from these homelands to the Celtiberian outposts on the Portuguese coast before sailing to their final point of destination—the American mainland.

Fell and I are no longer alone in our discovery of the ancient origins of Mystery Hill and many lesser sites in the United States. George Carter, Ph.D., the geographer of Texas A & M University, has been at Mystery Hill many times. Dr. Vincent Cassidy of the Akron University history department and Professor Ed Kealy of the Holy Cross University (Worcester, Massachusetts) history department are also among those who support the ancient origins of the area. Even so cautious a scientist as Dr. James Swanger of the Carnegie Museum of Natural History in Pittsburgh thinks that Mystery Hill is very ancient indeed.

In addition to my own and others' scholarly research, this present book also includes clues provided by touch psychometry. Ever since I introduced it in 1967 (in *Window to the Past*), historical verification through this technique has become a legitimate adjunct of archaeology. Far from being "occult," this system of deriving imprints of past events (like psychic photography) via sensitive individuals has been used by a number of recent researchers with gratifying results, and the American Society of Psychical Research has pursued regular experiments in this direction.

Prof. Hans Holzer, Ph.D
New York City
June 22, 1991

LONG BEFORE COLUMBUS

HOW THE ANCIENTS DISCOVERED AMERICA

THE ANCIENT MARINERS IN AMERICA

Relics from the past that cannot be explained on the basis of the current, officially sanctioned view of American history have been found all over the United States. At first, when some of these relics, such as the Kensington rune stone, were discovered, traditional archaeologists seemed to see only two choices: either they could explain the unorthodox finds as something else, something they were not, or they could declare them fakes. When the number of unusual finds and sites grew in the latter part of the nineteenth century and the early part of this century, it became no longer practicable to declare them all fakes. Perhaps the traditionalists assumed at this point that if they ignored the whole matter no one else would pay much attention either. But Americans are a curious lot, and newspapers, radio, and television have a way of making good stories out of unusual occurrences and unusual artifacts that turn up in the Americas. Also, local citizens may take up the cudgel for "their" special ruin or artifact and thus bring it to wider attention.

It stands to reason that if ancient mariners landed on American shores, they didn't restrict themselves to one tiny place. Also it makes sense that if people from one place arrived in America, then perhaps people from another place arrived around the same time or a little later. It has been proven time and again that ships built by the ancients were quite capable of traversing great distances and that navigation even at an early stage was capable of bringing people from the Old World to American shores. (See *Maps of the Ancient Sea Kings*, by Charles H. Hapgood, in which ocean voyages of the ancients are fully discussed.) The same ships that traveled from one end of the Mediterranean to the other were equally capable of traveling from Gibraltar to the Americas, as the distance is not that much greater. Yet this theory is still too radical for most established experts.

Colin Renfrew, the British archaeologist and anthropologist whose writings have appeared in *Scientific American* and *The American Journal of Archaeology*, stated it best in his book *Before Civilization*: "The study of prehistory today is in a state of crisis. Archaeologists all over the world have realized that much of prehistory, as written in the existing textbooks, is inadequate: some of it is quite simply wrong." Admitting that some errors are to be expected, but that the number of errors has risen to a height that is no longer excusable, he said, "So fundamental are these to the conventional view of the past that prehistorians in the United States refer to the various attempts to question them, to attempt the reconstruction of the past without them, as 'the New Archaeology.'"

Even radiocarbon dating has its limitations. This method of dating archaeological remains is based upon the phenomenon of high-energy cosmic rays reaching the Earth from outer space. When these rays strike the atmosphere, they break apart the nuclei of some atoms, releasing free neutrons. Whenever one of these free neutrons collides with the nucleus of a nitrogen atom, it is absorbed by the atom while a proton is released, changing the atom into radioactive carbon.

A stable nitrogen atom has a mass number of fourteen, its nucleus containing seven protons and seven neutrons. The addition of a neutron and the subtraction of a proton from this atom transforms it into a radioactive atom that is called carbon 14 because it also has a mass number of fourteen but contains eight neutrons and six protons and thus has the chemical properties of carbon.

This radiocarbon decays. When a living organism dies, no more radiocarbon enters it. This permits archaeologists to arrive at conclusions concerning the age of a sample by detecting the remaining radiocarbon in it. However, the method of dating samples by this calculation is limited: after about seventy thousand years of age, samples have very little radioactivity left in them, and their radiocarbon can no longer be measured. Thus the method is useless when it comes to archaeological samples that are more than seventy thousand years in age. Even with more recent samples, laboratory determination of the radioactivity is a delicate matter. Background radiation is always present in a laboratory, and various other factors (not the least of which is interpretation) make the radiocarbon dating method somewhat less than reliable.

Science writer John Keel also pointed out how little we really know about our own history: although we have a reasonably complete record of the last two thousand years and partial knowledge going back five thousand years, we have precious little beyond that. "We can't even be sure that the Egyptians built the pyramids," wrote Keel in *Strange Creatures from Time and Space.* "The pyramids may have already been in existence when the first Egyptian empire was founded, just as the great mounds of North and South America were already here when the first Indians arrived on the scene." Keel also spoke of the strange carvings on North American rocks, which can be clearly recognized only from the air:

> Many of the great mounds of Ohio, Minnesota, and Mississippi are in the form of serpents and elephants. The beasts have been extinct in North America for thousands of years. . . . From Florida to California there are also intricate patterns cut into the ground visible only from the air, just as the astounding Nazca lines of the Peruvian desert forming spiders, snakes, and other animals can be properly viewed only from an airplane.

Keel thought that high civilizations existed and somehow destroyed themselves or were destroyed. As the ancient cities fell into ruin, the cavemen then inherited the Earth.

> As men spread across the face of the planet, the places of those elders were rediscovered. Man's new-founded sciences couldn't fit such traces into their new concepts, however, so the evidence was ignored. As a result, the Earth has two histories: the history taught in our colleges and schools, and the real but ignored history of a very ancient people and of strange forces which have often supervised human events.

Amongst the unpalatable but true facts is the 1929 discovery in Constantinople of the Piri Reis Map. (See Hapgood's *Maps of the Ancient Sea Kings.*) This map, originally drawn in 1513, portrays the Earth in such a way that it could have been drawn only from an aerial survey. There is also the Yale Vinland Map, which was drawn fifty years before Columbus started out on his "discovery" voyage. Viking houses have been discovered on the Ungab Peninsula in northern Canada that date back to the eleventh and twelfth centuries. Iron utensils and weapons of European origin have been unearthed in Canada and Massachusetts.

When a stone inscribed with unusual letters was found in 1885 near Bat Creek, Tennessee, local antiquarians decided it had to be the work of Cherokee Indians. Fortunately, a more recent investigation of the stone by Dr. Joseph B. Mahan of the Museum of Arts and Crafts at Columbus, Georgia, discounted the "Indian theory"—that favorite formula for explaining away discoveries that do not fit in with traditionally accepted theories.

A similar stone was found by Manfred Metcalf at Fort Benning, Georgia, in 1968. Metcalf was looking for stones to build a barbecue grill in his backyard when he unearthed the stone. It was nine inches square and covered with triangles, circles, and straight and wavy lines. He passed it on to Dr. Mahan, who thought the markings appeared to be characteristically Mediterranean. Dr. Cyrus H. Gordon, chairman of Mediterranean studies at Brandeis University, agreed. There were strong similarities between the Metcalf stone and samples of Minoan writing dating back at least three thousand years, to the Bronze Age civilization that flourished on Crete from 3000 to 1100 B.C.

Strange carvings and paintings have also been found on walls of caves and rock shelters in southern Illinois. Mythological characters, the sun, the swastika, and animal life are among the depicted images. Irving Peithman, curator of archaeology at Southern Illinois University, told the Associated Press that "there is no tradition among living Indians to explain southern Illinois's earliest art works."

Betty Miller, a resident shopkeeper in the small town of Massillon, Ohio, brought a most unusual relic to my attention in 1970. A carved bit of iron ore, it had been exhibited at Massillon Museum since 1905 as an Ohioan Indian artifact. Its origins were now in question, with some supposition that it was actually a Norse rune stone dating back to A.D. 1154. The stone was first discovered in 1905 and later turned over to the Massillon Library as part of a collection donated by the late Dr. Abraham Per Lee Pease. The library then gave it to the museum. Pease had purchased the stone in 1880 from the family of Christian Spangler, although this man's name is written as Christian Palmer in the 1905 museum catalog.

The piece depicted what was interpreted as a carved face surmounted by what appeared to be some form of writing. A hard look at a photograph of the stone, however, gave me a totally different impression. To begin with, the stone did not look Norse at all to me, but instead resembled Mediterranean stones. What had appeared to be a woman's face seemed, in fact, to be the face of the sun surrounded on all sides by rays. But whether it was a Norse tombstone or an even more ancient artifact—how did it get to Massillon, Ohio?

The mysterious rune stone came to the attention of Dr. Clyde Keeler, a physician as well as a collector who had been searching for it for ten years. He wrote to the mayor of Massillon and inquired about the descendants of the Pease family, who might know about the stone. Later, in an interview published by the Massillon *Evening Independent*, Keeler described the stone as shaped like "a nodule of kidney."

Strange artifacts are constantly discovered in the United States, sometimes by simple farmers who have neither the know-how to do much about them nor the motivation to upset the theories of the archaeological establishment. For example, on October 24, 1969, I received a strange communication from M.J. Anderson of Washington State. Anderson had once visited a medium who had advised him that "something" was buried in the hills of his farm and that someday he would find it. Sure enough, while clearing some land in 1955, Anderson uncovered some "Stone Age artifacts." These were little figurines of birds and other animals of various kinds, even a rhinoceros head and the head of a man. The pieces were not in perfect condition—parts were missing here and there—but they were still clearly recognizable. There was also a sword, forty inches in length, the handle of which had been broken off, and two skinning knives. Anderson found these at an elevation of eleven hundred feet; he thinks that similar artifacts might have existed at a lower elevation in the area but that the glaciers carried most of them out to sea.

Frank Glynn was assistant U.S. postmaster at Clinton, Connecticut, when he became interested in one of the strangest archaeological puzzles in the United States. This puzzle involves a crude effigy outlined on the surface of a rock, apparently executed with blows from an iron worker's tools. The six-foot-tall figure wears a helmet and flowing cloak like that of a medieval knight, grasps a dagger in his right hand and a decorated shield in his left, and has an oversized sword hanging from his belt. Glynn stated in an early 1970s New England Antiquities Research Association (NEARA) newsletter:

> The existence of artificial decoration on an exposed ledge beside an old trail leading off Westford Hill in Massachusetts has been a matter of written record since at least 1883. Search and inquiry have failed to produce evidence of other than the one native tradition printed in

1883—that the inscription is of Indian origin and represents a twenty-inch-long, stick-figured "old Indian" looking out across the wide panorama of open country to the northwest.

In 1946, W.B. Goodwin published two photographs and a line drawing of the "knight of Westford Hill." At that time, only the sword was visible on the rock; the remainder of the figure was covered with dirt. Goodwin interpreted the figure as an eleventh-century Norseman, because he recognized the sword as the type used in medieval Europe.

Glynn, however, dated the figure to the thirteenth and fourteenth centuries, two hundred years after the Vikings. England's historian Professor Lethbridge suggested to Glynn that he look for something more than the sword that was then visible on the rock. He even sent Glynn a drawing of a medieval knight and wrote, "Strip back the dirt and see if you don't see something like this." Glynn enthusiastically began uncovering the remainder of the image. It took him from 1952 to 1954 to remove four inches of dirt at the top and bottom of the image, but his labors were rewarded when the figure of the medieval knight appeared in full. Sure enough, it looked exactly like the drawing Professor Lethbridge had sent from Cambridge. Even details of the shield were visible and were sent to England for further study.

Now that Glynn and Lethbridge knew there was an authentic drawing of a fourteenth-century English knight on a Massachusetts hill, they were able to look through historical records to see if there was any mention of an early European voyage to North American shores. In particular, the presence of a round brooch, a star and crescent, and a small boat with furled sails on the knight's shield promised some sort of identification. Their research turned up Harry Sinclair, the Earl of Orkney, who led a fourteenth-century exploring party of Scottish noblemen to the western Atlantic. The same brooch that appears in the Westford Hill knight's shield also appears in the shields of several branches of the Orkney family, clearly indicating that the exploring party of fourteenth-century noblemen did indeed reach the New World, two hundred years before Columbus.

In 1961, Charles Michael Boland, considered by many the leading authority on prehistory in North America, wrote a major work on pre-Columbian discoveries of America entitled *They All Discovered America*. In the preface, Boland said:

This book is about the numberless people who discovered and rediscovered America in the 2,000 years before Columbus. While there are doubtless more than the 19 groups whose adventures are related here, I have chosen to dwell only on those whose explorations have been documented in histories other than our own, or whose penetration of North and South America provided tangible, archaeological evidence of their visits.

According to Boland, the first discoverers of America were of Asiatic background. They came to America over the Bering land bridge sometime between 35,000 and 18,000 B.C. This information is supported by Paleolithic finds including both human bones and tools, clearly of foreign origin, which date back to the period indicated by Boland. These finds undermined the conventional view that the "Indians" came to the Western Hemisphere sometime around 3500 B.C.

Boland gave no news of any further incursions from the Old World until the Phoenicians arrived between 480 and 146 B.C.:

> The second discoverer of America arrived in ship from the Mediterranean, and left a record of his visit in a rubble of stones on a New Hampshire hillside. . . . He came leading a mournful band of religious freedom seekers during the first millennium before the birth of Christ. Others of his kind came at later times, but for different reasons, and they in turn left records of their visits in scattered stones and ruins near the banks of the Susquehanna in Pennsylvania, and on steaming jungle rocks, deep in Brazil.

The way Boland described it, there weren't any landfalls prior to the Phoenicians, who arrived around 480 B.C. at the earliest. This leaves a long period of history and an even longer period of prehistory totally devoid of any contact between the Old World and the New World. Is this likely, however, to have been the case?

Professor Charles H. Hapgood of Keene State College of the University of New Hampshire, author of the magnificent account of ancient mariners *Maps of the Ancient Sea Kings: Evidence of Advanced Civilization in the Ice Age*, carefully weighed the available evidence of archaeology, linguistics, and comparative mythology. He came to the conclusion that

> the evidence for an ancient worldwide civilization, or a civilization that for a considerable time must have dominated much of the world in a very remote period, is rather plentiful—at least potentially. We have manifold leads which further research can hardly fail to develop.

In his notes amended to the book, Professor Hapgood spoke of a colleague, Professor A.W. Brogger, a specialist in the field of ancient deep sea navigation, who

> thinks . . . deep sea navigation may have been at its height as much as 3,000 years before Christ, and . . . on the decline after 1500 B.C. so that the very period which we used to select as the beginning of real seamanship, the Phoenician, is shown as having been at the bottom of the curve, which thereafter rose slowly until it attained a new high in the navigation cycle in the Viking age, which started less than 1,500 years ago. That a man of the Old World discovered the Americas from Brazil to Greenland, during Brogger's golden age of navigation 5,000 years ago, and perhaps earlier, rests merely on possibilities and probabilities. As yet we cannot prove it certain, though we can prove it likely.

If one is to follow Boland's reasoning, there is evidence pointing to three general categories of visitors before Columbus. There was, first of all, the ancient Phoenician group, of which I will speak more when I discuss the origin of Mystery Hill. According to Boland, there was large-scale migration between the Mediterranean and North America as a result of occasional and largely accidental forays by individual Phoenician ships into the Western Hemisphere. Upon safe return to their homeland, these sailors provided the Phoenicians with sure knowledge of land to the west of Gibraltar. Boland relates:

> Some strayed from the plotted course and came to the Chesapeake, whence they sailed north up the Susquehanna River to settle in what is now Pennsylvania. Others strayed even more and sailed to the coast of South America.

Hundreds of stones inscribed with letters of the Phoenician alphabet were found near Mechanicsburg, Pennsylvania. Boland thinks they were part of a ruined temple that stood there at one time. Over eighty years ago, a strange piece of dark stone about the size of a chocolate bar was found in a grave at Bat Creek in Loudon County, Tennessee. On it was carved ancient Hebrew writing that Cyrus Gordon deciphered to read, "For the land of Judah, the year one." Nine human skeletons were also found in the grave in which the stone was discovered. In support of the genuineness of this artifact is the Metcalf stone, which archaeologist Joseph Mahan of the Columbus, Georgia, Museum of Arts and Crafts had sent to Cyrus Gordon; this stone also bears an ancient Hebrew inscription. In addition, there are three coins portraying the leader of the Jewish rebels in the Second Revolt of the Jews (A.D. 136-137), Simon Bar Kochba, that were dug up at three different sites in Kentucky between 1937 and 1967.

Another stone found in Brazil in 1872 bears an ancient Canaanite text indicating that those who carved the stone were subjects of King Hiram III, who reigned over Phoenicia from 553 to 533 B.C. In 1823, the chief justice of the Supreme Court of Tennessee, John Haywood, found Roman coins in the ground near Bat Creek, Tennessee; they had been minted by second-century emperor Antoninus Pius, his son Marcus Aurelius, and Aurelius' son Commodus. However, because these finds were made by enthusiastic amateurs rather than establishment archaeologists, the suspicion of fakery was immediately attached to them, regardless of their true circumstances.

Boland's second general category of pre-Columbian visitors was the Roman group. He reported on and published photographs of "mysterious symbols" carved on a rock in Brunswick County, Virginia. He ascribed these symbols to a Roman origin of about A.D. 64. Boland also compared an ancient bronze cup found in Virginia with similar ones discovered at Pompeii that are now in the Museum of Naples. All over Virginia, Roman nails and iron utensils have been found in undisturbed sites. These artifacts in no way give the impression of being fake.

Boland continued his history of European travelers to American shores with the journey of Saint Brendan in A.D. 551, but he stated, "Brendan's visit to America was not the first by monks from Erin's shore, nor was it the last." This is the third general category of pre-Columbian visitors he discussed. In A.D. 982, a band of Irish monks came to American in order to escape the pagan Vikings who were then ravaging their homeland. They founded colonies known as Greater Ireland, which still existed when the Vikings themselves came over and began to settle in the eastern United States. Called the Celi Dei, or Culdees, these pre-Saint Patrick Christians of Ireland led austere lives that made it possible for them to survive in the wilderness and amongst hostile Indians. Ruins of their dwellings and artifacts attributable to ninth- and tenth-century Ireland have been found all over New England, including Massachusetts and New Hampshire, the site of Mystery Hill.

About the same time, toward the end of the tenth century, the Vikings also started to explore America. At first, they drifted toward it with the prevailing winds. Later, they arrived in an organized manner when they realized that there was much land beyond Iceland and Greenland. Evidence of their presence in the United States has been found not only in the eastern coastal areas but as far inland as Minnesota and along the Mississippi River. A rock inscribed with a runic inscription dating from the tenth century was discovered in Bourne, Massachusetts. Another rock was found at Assonet Neck, Rhode Island, but its inscription has been only partially deciphered. An eleventh-century inscribed rune stone was found at Yarmouth, Nova Scotia. The famous Old Stone Tower at Newport, Rhode Island, which tourist guides like to date to "colonial times," is, in the opinion of Boland, the work of a twelfth-century Icelandic bishop. The so-called Kensington rune stone, discovered in 1898 at Kensington, Minnesota, and now securely dated to the fourteenth century, had been attacked as a fake but was eventually validated by many responsible archaeologists.

Utensils of iron and stone have been found in graves and settlement sites all the way from Canada to the southern waters of the Mississippi River and from Cape Cod to Minnesota. Few contemporary scholars would contradict the Vikings' presence in the United States long before Columbus, but most school children are still told that Columbus discovered America. Ultimately, new generations of textbooks will have to tell history as it really was, not as it was created in the minds of nineteenth- and early twentieth-century conformers who settled down to a comfortable life with Columbus and ignored evidence to the contrary.

Why are Americans so adamant in declaring Columbus our one and only true discoverer, allowing only an occasional mention of Amerigo Vespucci, whose first name gave America its name? To make things worse, Columbus didn't even reach the boundaries of the current United States; he reached some islands at a considerable distance from the coast and called them the New World. He knew perfectly well that he hadn't reached India, yet those islands are still called the West Indies.

What these oversights are perpetuating is, in fact, nothing more than hidden colonialism. This colonial spirit, which motivated Columbus to make his westward voyage and which founded the Spanish-speaking colonies to the south and the English-language colonies in most of the United States, insists on perpetuating the myth that the civilized races of western

Europe came to America to teach the heathen savages and save them from the misery of their own culture.

This hidden colonialism is solidly based on a kind of brutal expansionist Christianity inherited from the Middle Ages. From the viewpoint of this Christian colonialism, it would be a shame if non-Christian races, especially from non-western European stock, were responsible for the initial contacts between the Old World and the New World. After all, when Americans teach Spanish colonial history, we tell our young how the brave conquistadores came to America, despite the perils of the sea, to "enlighten" the native population, bring them the blessings of Christianity and civilization, and teach them how to be good, obedient citizens.

As Americans, we do not tell our children that the people who came with and followed Columbus were nothing more than scavengers solely bent on exploiting the native population. Those of the native elements whom they could not exterminate, they enslaved. We do not report the refined tortures inflicted upon a nation used to kindness and goodness. We do not speak much about the attempted extermination of the American Indian by the British colonists and their successors, the American pioneers. We do, in fact, present a distorted image of the truth.

On the other end of the historical scale, modern people also hold on to a strange view of ancient society. We cling to the idea of an orderly progression of knowledge: that ancient people attained certain levels of knowledge that were altered and in some measure obscured in the Middle Ages but then once more vivified during the Renaissance and, of course, vastly improved upon by modern times. We ignore, as much as we can, the fact that certain scientific knowledge was known to ancient people but has been lost and never rediscovered. What of it? the traditional scientists seem to say. So what if Egyptian graves yield surgical instruments comparable in fineness and quality to modern equipment created for the same purpose? So what if the people who built Stonehenge had astronomical knowledge comparable to ours of a scant few years ago? As long as historians believe that people started out in caves and then progressively mounted the ladder of knowledge to reach the present "pinnacle," an essential portion of the truth will be ignored.

Prior to humanity's cave-dwelling status, there must have existed high civilizations that were destroyed either by outside forces or by rivalry amongst themselves. The evidence for this existence of high-level prehistoric civilizations is mounting daily. No longer can it be ignored. Charles Berlitz, in his memorable *Mysteries from Forgotten Worlds*, gave factual evidence for the existence of such civilizations, including photographs. I discussed with him the stubbornness of most establishment archaeologists when confronted with evidence contrary to their ingrained beliefs. "If I showed them the ruins of a city at the bottom of the sea, off the Atlantic Coast," Berlitz commented, "they would probably say, 'Oh, that is just a shipload of ancient Greek masonry that sank.'"

This attitude is one more example of Procrustes, the legendary monster of Greek mythology who forced travelers to sleep in his bed. If the travelers were too long, he cut off their feet; if they were too short, he stretched them. One way or the other, they had to conform to the size of his bed. Similarly, whatever the archaeological facts, if they do not conform to the preconceived notions of the archaeological establishment, they are either called false, misinterpreted, or assumed not to exist. Damn the evidence—full speed ahead to obsolete teachings!

It is against this background that one must view the continuing discovery of evidence in North America that points to the presence of ancient European cultures where none were thought to be. Granted, some accommodations are being made by the archaeological community with respect to the Norse people because the evidence is so overwhelming. Even in this case, however, cries of "fake" are usually the establishment's initial reaction to discoveries of rune stones or other artifacts in remote areas of the United States. The Kensington rune stone is a good case in point: the poor farmer who found it eventually became so disgusted with the accusations of fakery that he used it as a doorstop for his barn. Ultimately, he contributed his share to a better understanding of history by allowing a less prejudiced researcher to have it. Thus the rune stone was rehabilitated and translated.

It is pretty well known that people from Scandinavia traveled across North America as far west as Minnesota. Remnants of their voyages have been found in the Midwest, even along the Mississippi River and in the southern states—great distances from the coastal areas. This is not surprising: the Vikings were superb sailors, and their longboats were as suitable for traveling up rivers as for transocean voyages. Also, perhaps the idea of a Scandinavian discovery of America is less controversial because the Vikings were, after all, Christians, albeit newly converted.

Then, too, there is abundant documentation, not the least of which is the saga of Eric the Red. In this saga, his voyages are described in great detail. Ever since Viking artifacts have been uncovered, the saga has been taken more seriously; it turned out that the chronicler was, after all, telling the truth.

I am concerned in this book primarily with the North American continent and not with the evidence for early European contact with South America, although such contact has also been abundantly proven through artifacts and inscribed stones found in the far inland reaches of South America. There is, in addition, evidence of ancient European faces, art forms, alphabets, and decorations in the arts and crafts of the Latin American population before the arrival of Columbus. The races who set out beyond the Pillars of Hercules would naturally have reached South America and North America—not necessarily of their own volition, but because of the winds. There is no doubt that they had the capability of traveling: ancient navigation had achieved a very high skill level by the time the Roman state began to rise. I would go so far as to state that any and all ancient peoples who had ships capable of sailing the Mediterranean would have attempted to sail the Atlantic, and probably did.

The evidence is fairly clear with respect to the known races of Europe: the Phoenicians and Minoans of Crete came to North America, as did the Romans and the early Irish. These are the known nationalities, with whose cultures modern people are familiar, allowing us comparative studies involving their artifacts. But what of the strange, giant markings on the ground, which make sense only when viewed from the air, that have been discovered in the highlands of Peru and elsewhere? Erich von Däniken described these as markers and landing fields for astronauts from other worlds. They may be just that, unless there was once a super race on Earth itself, capable of using the air as a means of travel.

Von Däniken's disclosure of these runways and aerial markings is common knowledge now, yet there are similar markings in the United States that are unknown to the general public. In Colorado, for instance, huge but faint markings have been discovered on the land that make no sense whatsoever when seen from a ground-level perspective. As soon as one is airborne, however, these tracings take on the shape of "runways" and other orderly designs. It is interesting that such designs are found both in the highlands of Peru and in the Rocky Mountains, suggesting that high points with plateaus were chosen by their creators for practical reasons. Surely, if space travelers came to South America, they could have come to North America as well.

Still another problem with unraveling the mysteries presented by pre-Columbian visitors in the United States is that of separating the different layers of occupation at a given site. It is almost an axiom that advantageous landmarks appealed to more than one visitor and were used over and over again by different people at various times. Stonehenge, for instance, was built by the ancient Britons. It was later taken over by the Druids, who made certain alterations, and still later by the successors to the Druids living under the Romans. Eventually it was passed to the Anglo-Saxons. In the case of Troy, as many as eleven layers of occupation have been unearthed.

Christian churches were frequently built on the exact spots where pagan sanctuaries had stood for long periods of time, because such sites were considered psychically active and, from a religious point of view, desirable. Strong locations usually have such long histories of previous occupation. Even buildings have been located on the identical spots as previous structures. King Arthur, a very real historical person who lived in the early sixth century as a post-Roman regional ruler, built Camelot on the foundations of a Roman fortification. As I will show in later chapters, Mystery Hill presents such a complex picture as well, for it is a desirably elevated location that seems to have appealed to a succession of visitors.

The origin of at least some of the visitors to North America is a tantalizing question. We Americans can easily assimilate the presence of ancient Phoenicians and Greeks, even if it goes against the grain of what we were taught in school, because these, at least, were people with whose cultures we are reasonably familiar. We can easily imagine how some of these ancients drifted by chance to American shores, then managed to travel inland a bit before they died. But what about the people who carved the giant signs into the North American landscape—the same people who carved markers into the hillsides of England and France and Scandinavia—carvings that make absolutely no sense in terms of terrestrial use?

I myself have stood on a tiny segment of one such marker, known as the Long Man of Wilmington, in southern England. Even from far away, even from a few hundred feet up, the figure makes no sense, though from higher in the air it can be recognized as the outline of a man. For the purpose of terrestrial use, the unknown carvers might just as well have made the figure 1 percent of its actual size and still have satisfied whatever usage this marker might have been put to by the people in the area.

It cannot be assumed that the ancient Phoenicians or Greeks carved these giant figures, nor that they used them, for to what use could they have put these enormous figures? To walk upon them is hazardous, as they are usually in inaccessible parts of mountains. Some historians suggest that they were used as expressions of divine worship, yet the figures do not jibe with the deity concepts of the people involved. The fact that these carvings are truly gigantic in size, and painted white to boot, inevitably leads to the conclusion that they were meant not for people on Earth but for someone approaching Earth from a distance. They are, in fact, just as von Däniken says, aerial markers, used in aerial navigation by ships of an unknown character.

Since this aspect of archaeology is almost completely ignored by most responsible archaeologists, research has been slow and left to enthusiastic amateurs. In the middle 1980s, a team under the direction of West Coast archaeologist and New Age pioneer Frederick McLaurin Adams completed charting and measuring a number of such large markings in the Colorado mountains. There must be countless others scattered across the United States that are still undiscovered.

The method known as psychometry, in which human sensitives are "let loose" on mysterious or puzzling sites to pick up impressions from their past histories, is both respectable and frequently successful. I demonstrated the effectiveness of psychometry in my book *Windows to the Past*, in which I recounted how it had been used to pinpoint the exact site of the Cape Cod landfall of the Vikings, find the true location of Camelot in southern England, and even reconstruct the true background of President Lincoln's assassination. Much new material was revealed that was later verified and corroborated through conventional documentary sources. Psychometry, then, is another way of determining the past of any given archaeological site, provided one has the patience to undertake it and the access to the proper psychics to help with the research. This I have done, as later chapters of this work will indicate.

Nancy Hamilton, writing about psychic tools for archaeology in the weekly newspaper *Psychic News*, remarked that "from time to time, psychic gifts have influenced archaeological work. Such helps as dreams, clairvoyance, astral projection, and memory recall of the past have been used in seeking answers to man's history." Miss Hamilton mentions the medium Anna Caterina Emmerick, a German peasant woman whose visions of the life of Jesus were used by Clemens Brentano as the basis of his history of Jesus. These visions led to verification in strange and often dramatic ways.

> Among the detailed descriptions given by Sister Emmerick was one of the house at Ephesus to which John took Jesus' mother in her later years. In 1891, two Lazarist priests from Smyrna wanted to check the authenticity of the account. After a five-day search they came to a small ruin on an isolated peak south of the ancient city. The site and the floor plan corresponded accurately with Sister Emmerick's description. The priests also learned that descendents of early Christians of Ephesus had called the ruin the house of the holy virgin and for many years had made annual pilgrimages there on the Feast of the Assumption. Later archaeological studies of the site showed that the foundation of the original house was dated from the first century. Nearby were found the remains of a Christian cave settlement and a palace ruin as described by Sister Emmerick.

However, "psychic archaeology" can occasionally be a mixed blessing, as is perhaps best illustrated by the claim of Moebus Society's Stephen Schwartz and his associates to have discovered "Cleopatra's Palace" at the bottom of Alexandria's harbor. What they did find were the remnants of a Roman mansion of the first century B.C. Exciting as the discovery was, subsequent work at the site has not proven it to be Cleo's old hangout.

Today, there are new tools, new ways of probing the past—not just radiocarbon dating or other chemical analyses. I am in favor of using the latest technology available, as long as it is not proclaimed to be the absolute and final word. For example, the Shroud of Turin may be older than people think when the matter of scientific and ecclesiastical politics is taken into account with respect to its recent "investigation" by a team of scientists.

While researchers are developing tools and perhaps becoming a bit more open-minded about the possibilities of pre-Columbian visitors to America, preciously little work is actually being done in this area along so-called "unorthodox" lines. The search for Atlantis occurs mainly in books and magazines, and no money seems to be available for serious, unbiased professionals to follow up on the persistent presence of pre-Christian artifacts in America derived from European and Mediterranean sources.

For example, Alexander von Wuthenau's profusely illustrated work, *Unexpected Faces in Ancient America*, cannot be dismissed as meaningless or a "coincidence" (if there be such a thing). Written in 1975, it is still, alas, a rare book. If a picture is worth ten thousand words, von Wuthenau's tome is a treasury of knowledge indeed. It has long been the habit of conventionally trained researchers in archaeology to dismiss as "counterfeit" or "questionable" anything not conforming to the currently accepted knowledge about the flow of history. They've got a lot to learn.

I do not for a moment advocate the indiscriminate use of psychic abilities for rewriting history or proving the presence of ancient peoples where none have been hitherto proven. But I do recommend the use of sensitives or mediums, under careful test conditions, for researching suspected historical sites. This should be done with the understanding that whatever material is obtained be fully corroborated and researched in the conventional ways of historical and archaeological research. In other words, let psychics be the "bloodhounds" who ferret out clues from the past, clues that otherwise might remain hidden to even the most well-trained archaeologist. Only in combining archaeological methodology with the wider horizons of parapsychology can we hope to unravel some of the remaining mysteries of our past.

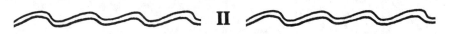

II

From Pattee's Caves to Mystery Hill

There are perhaps a dozen recognized sites in North America where artifacts from the past have been found that could not be attributed to either local Indians or early Spaniards. However, none of them, not even the most startling Norse finds, compare to the stately appearance of a partially excavated sanctuary known today as Mystery Hill. Temples and important buildings of one kind or another have probably existed throughout history in various parts of the United States, but thus far none of them have been unearthed. Therefore, Mystery Hill stands in isolated splendor as a mysterious witness to a remote past.

Mystery Hill lies in the woods near North Salem, New Hampshire, a few miles from the Massachusetts border. It encompasses twenty acres of ground. Actually, the sanctuary itself occupies the highest part of a hill, but there are signs of building activity extending for at least two miles in all directions. Recently, additional excavations have shown that the entire hill was used as a very large observatory, with monoliths or dolmens (two or more upright stones supporting horizontal slabs) indicating certain positions of the sun. In order to see all that presently remains of the ancient sanctuary, one must walk a considerable distance from the center of it, which indicates that this was by no means a small, local temple but a major site.

By car, one reaches Mystery Hill by turning off Route 3 and following a winding country road halfway up the hill. There the road stops in front of a handsome, log cabin-type house. This is the administration building of the New England Antiquities Research Association (NEARA), which maintains the site. In this comfortable building there are displays of artifacts unearthed at the site, drawings and maps of reconstructions, and display cases of research material and publications pertinent to Mystery Hill. But the building is not only a small museum; it also serves as a kind of country store and souvenir shop. All funds taken in at this little shop go toward one goal: to dig further into the site of Mystery Hill and to restore as much of it as possible to its former appearance. During the summer season, there are volunteer guides available to take tourists up to the crest of the hill and explain the various excavations.

From the administration building, one walks uphill for ten minutes along rough but well-marked paths. Upon coming to the top of the hill, one reaches a rough plateau extending a good distance north and east.

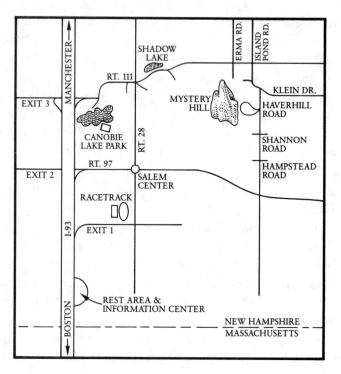

Figure 1. *Road map to Mystery Hill.*

Here the various ruins are carefully segregated, connected by pathways, and numbered. Every visitor is handed a simple guide and map by which he or she can identify the various buildings. In case tourist guides are not available, speakers playing tape-recorded explanations are tied to trees.

The top of the hill is well lit, though few tourists come after hours. Evidently there were no trees on the hill at the time the sanctuary was first built, but the site has since become enshrouded in dense forest. The administration is trying hard to remove at least some of the trees in the immediate vicinity of the buildings in order to restore the majesty of this elevation, which in its prime would have been visible from as far away as the sea. To travelers approaching from the seashore in ancient times, this rise of lands must have been an awesome sight.

Under President Robert Stone, the administration of NEARA has named the various buildings and ruins, sometimes based on the supposed function a building might have served, sometimes based on images a ruin suggests. Until about two years ago, there were thirty-nine separate archaeological sites known at Mystery Hill. Today there are several more known in outlying areas of the hill, principally monoliths set up as markers for astronomical purposes.

As one leaves the administration building, the first building encountered is the Watch House. According to Stone, it was perhaps used to watch over a procession going up the hill along the double-walled Processional Path. However, the building may also have been used for storage, living quarters, or even as a tomb. Over two hundred similar structures have been located by NEARA in other places in New England.

Next, one encounters the Processional Path, which connects the Watch House to the main complex atop the hill. In the wall directly below the sanctuary is the twelve-foot-deep Lower Well, which, due to its water level, has never been fully excavated. Stone points out that the inclusion of wells in walls is an ancient custom that was totally alien to the colonial period in America. Directly opposite the Lower Well, NEARA unearthed a gigantic clay deposit in 1969. There is a large fire pit nearby that is believed to have been used for the making of pottery. Stone wonders whether the existence of the clay pit may have induced the ancient builders to select Mystery Hill as the place for their temples.

At the Lower Well, one turns right, and the path leads to what Stone calls the lower gate to the main site (see photo 1). Here one encounters a "modern artifact"—a heavy wire fence erected by a former owner of the site, William Goodwin. On the other side of it, one passes a charcoal pit excavated in 1968 and proceeds to the Well of the Crystals. In 1963, Stone and his associates dug up some quartz crystals in this well. Their origin was proven to be a natural vertical intrusion in the bedrock, twenty-two feet down. One of these rough crystals was later psychometrized by one of my sensitives. Here the trail turns slightly to the left and passes the Sundial Rock. It portrays a crudely carved circle with a hole in its middle that Stone takes to be an ancient sun symbol.

Directly opposite the Sundial Rock is an underground shelter called the Megaron House (see photo 2). A megaron is a building surrounding a central courtyard. This one served as a shelter during the occupancy of the first recorded owner of the site, Jonathan Pattee. Outside the shelter is the Megaron Courtyard, a walled-in area utilized by Pattee, who lived on the hill from 1823 to 1849. Pattee used this particular area as a cellar and patched up some of the supporting walls. The difference between his masonry and that of the original structure is glaringly evident. In the course of his adaptation, Pattee also blocked off an ancient stairway, which, however, was rediscovered in 1959 by Frank Glynn, first chief archaeologist for the New England Antiquities Research Association.

Proceeding further up the hill along the pathway, one passes a site called Pattee's Fireplace, an earlier structure utilized by Pattee. Next, one comes to a ruined chamber with a roof slab weighing about six tons lying on the ground. It was here that several inscribed stones were discovered by members of NEARA in 1968 and 1969. They are now on display in the museum located in the administration building. Another giant manmade slab can be seen opposite this chamber as one proceeds downhill toward an "undetermined structure," only part of which is preserved.

Many of the stones from this site were carried off in the nineteenth century by stone robbers for use in their own buildings in the area. Since the archaeological site had no protection whatever until NEARA took over, valuable material disappeared over the years, making proper identification difficult in some instances.

Even further down the path stands another large structure, possibly once used as a dwelling of some sort. At this point, the path retraces itself, winding around this structure and passing through cutouts, or spaces of various sizes, that Stone surmises to have carried a religious connotation. Evidently, the original builders of the sanctuary had some problems with rain, for there are many drains cut into the bedrock.

Moving along the path, one then comes to a small shrine cut out of the bedrock on the left. The historical use of this altar is presently unknown, although Stone suggests that it was used for fertility rites for

the growth of crops. Across from it is a large structure that NEARA calls
The Pulpit. Much of the material is missing from it and, according to
Stone, may be found as curbstones in the nearby cities of Andover and
Lawrence, Massachusetts.

Further on, past minor evidence of other man-made structures and
activities, one reaches the compound itself, which occupies the largest
part of the plateau. There are several buildings here, one of which is called
the V Hut, so named for its shape. Stone surmises that this structure had
some important role to play because there is a kind of "holy water" basin
cut into the bedrock on the left side of it. Right next to it is the Tomb
of Lost Souls, used to hold cremation ashes. The tomb was sealed off with
large stone slabs, which are now missing.

Directly below the tomb and in the center of the area is the Mensal
Stone, a bedrock slab weighing fourteen tons that Stone believes was used
in ancient fertility rites. Next to it, there is an area that was used for cremation of the dead, as is indicated by the many rocks in the wall that
have been badly burned. Behind this cremation bed, there is the avenue
leading to the Oracle Chamber, one of the highlights of the hill. This
avenue or passageway is thought to have been the site of one or perhaps
two chambers. To the right of it is an excavation that NEARA considers
one of the most important in the area. Robert Stone commented in the
Journal of the New England Antiquities Research Association:

> As viewed, this archaeological excavation is not very impressive, yet
> the results have perhaps made it the most important part of the site,
> as thus far three radiocarbon dates have been produced from here.
> Rotted pine roots found in the walls in 1967 were dated to the year
> 1690, proving that the walls were there prior to Mr. Pattee's occupan-
> cy. In 1969, at two to four inches above bedrock, charcoal that had
> sifted into the walls was found below these roots and dated to 3,000
> years ago. Then in 1971, a third and even older date of 1525 B.C. was
> obtained. It should be noted that the top layer of bedrock was quar-
> ried and used in the site's construction, indicating that this charcoal
> sifted in after the site's construction.

North of the passageway is the Oracle Chamber itself, probably one
of the most important structures at the entire site. The chamber is entered
by a flight of stairs that go down a short passage (see photo 3). According to photographs, this passage was covered by large roof slabs in 1915,
but it is presently without them. The elongated chamber itself is well

drained by small channels grooved into the bedrock floor; to this very day, the drainage system works. The floor slants slightly toward the center, so that if one descends into the chamber, one reaches the lowest level at its midpoint.

Figure 2. *Oracle Chamber, looking toward fireplace and chimney flue above. Drawing by Angela Werneke.*

It is exactly in the center of the chamber that a so-called speaking tube is located at the height of an average person's chin (see photo 4). This tube allowed a person to be heard outside the Oracle Chamber in the vicinity of the so-called Sacrificial Table, which is located just outside the chamber. The effect was that the table itself appeared to be doing the speaking. Such devices were well-known to the ancient Greek oracles.

To this day, the speaking tube at Mystery Hill is in operating condition, but the administration does not encourage the spreading of this fact, for they do not wish to induce visiting tourists to use it for their own purposes. Directly below the speaking tube is a niche large enough for a human being to crawl into and yet be completely hidden from view. Such a person would be in a position to observe the activity within the chamber through a small opening near the floor.

At the far end of the underground chamber, there is an opening in the roof that seems to have once contained two stone louvers that could be opened and closed. There was also a large slab that slid on stone tracks for the purpose of closing the flue. In the center of the chamber, roughly

Figure 3. *Ibex or running deer in wall of Oracle Chamber.*

opposite the speaking tube, there is a primitive seat hewn from bedrock. Leading past it, there is a descending passage that is roughly two-thirds the length of the main chamber. Hewn into the right wall of this passage, there is another niche, and opposite it, in the left wall, there is a carving representing a running deer or ibex. This was discovered in the 1930s.

Further down this descending passage is another small niche containing an altar, large enough to have held a lamp. Underneath is an underground drain extending about forty-five feet (see photo 5). Excavations at the opposite end of this drain revealed a bend of ninety degrees in the drain cut into the bedrock; however, no artifacts of any importance were found in the area. Opposite it is a second egress from the chamber (see photo 7).

To the north of the Oracle Chamber are the remnants of another structure called the Sacrificial Pen by the archaeologists working on the site. They believe that animals meant for sacrifice were kept in stalls within that structure. Today, only the pen's floor, which is also partially the roof of the Oracle Chamber, and some of the pen's side walls are still standing.

To the west of the Oracle Chamber is the much-publicized Sacrificial Table (see photos 8, 9, 10). This is a four-and-a-half-ton grooved slab believed to have been used for sacrifices. This purpose was assumed not only because the slab is located in the exact center of the sanctuary, but also because it is the largest single stone slab of the site, and the speaking tube of the oracle leads directly to it. The grooves that follow the rectangular shape of the slab are considered drainage grooves for blood. Immediately below the slab is what Stone calls the Viewing Ramp because here, in the exact center of the site, one has the best vantage point for viewing the entire area.

The sanctuary proper is now surrounded by a wire fence that is locked up at night. Beyond it, however, the astronomical alignment monoliths extend a considerable distance. Nearly all the monoliths have been excavated, allowing the archaeologists working on the site to reconstruct the observatory aspects of the hill. In this regard, Mystery Hill has great similarities with England's Stonehenge, such as the dolmens marking the summer and winter solstices and the two equinoxes. Stone and his associates have tested this astronomical alignment repeatedly and found it to be very exact indeed. However, there are additional monoliths, the purpose of which is not yet entirely understood.

The Mystery Hill compound is by no means unique in New England, however. Only its state of preservation makes it stand out, since nearly all similar finds are either less spectacular or they merely consist of artifacts found in the ground. In a survey of what he called the "New England megalithic culture," Stone wrote in the New Hampshire Archaeological Society papers for October 1968, "Above- and below-ground stone structures continually being found in the northeastern section of North America, particularly in New England, have not, as of this date, been slotted into any particular time period of our history or prehistory." Adding that these sites were being methodically researched by local archaeological societies, Stone expressed his belief that "due to the increasing number of finds, [he] and many others are beginning to believe the answer to these stone structures lies in a megalithic period of time two to four thousand years B.C."

Stone admitted that the existence of a megalithic culture in the United States had not previously been accepted by the majority of archaeologists. NEARA had been comparing the North American structures with megalithic structures and monoliths still in existence at Stonehenge in England, Carnac in France, Malta in the Mediterranean, and even at locations in Scandinavia and Africa. They had found that there were great similarities between these stone structures of the Old World and those of the northeastern United States.

Deploring the fact that the existing structures in the United States were being referred to as "colonial root cellars" or "burial tombs or vaults" and that they were being relegated to well-known periods in U.S. history, Stone pointed out that neither colonial builders nor American Indians would have been capable of erecting the structures found, not to mention the fact that there were great similarities between the American structures and their European cousins. Although the complex at Mystery Hill is the largest in the area, a second one is located in Connecticut that contains a similar complicated pattern of walls and a double-ring stone circle. Its slabs protrude from the ground about one foot, but as the site is owned by a youth center, the land has thus far been untouched.

Another site exists at Webster, Massachusetts, but of the five scattered buildings once existing, only one remains. There is no official recognition of the importance of these structures, so the established archaeological and historical societies pay them no attention. Consequently, they are not protected from either vandals or those legal vandals known as builders. "The once famous Hill of Cairns in Bolton, Massachusetts. . . is also among the missing after new Interstate Highway 495 swept through it. . . . One of the cairns, which originally numbered in the hundreds, can still be seen from the highway," wrote Stone.

NEARA's count of dolmens stood at nine, with three more possibilities, at the time Stone made his report on the Hill of Cairns in 1968. Since then, additional ones have been found. "Monoliths and cairns have become so numerous that it has not been possible to keep abreast of them," he said.

Elsewhere in Massachusetts, NEARA recorded five large and unexplained grooved slabs similar to the so-called Sacrificial Table at Mystery Hill. Another one, found at Old Sturbridge Village, Massachusetts, had previously been moved from a site in Rhode Island. Still another, now in the farm museum in Hadley, Massachusetts, originally came from a site near the Quabbin Reservoir. Another such stone, removed from a Massachusetts hillside, is now in the museum of the city of New York, and one that was originally on Mount Shaw in New Hampshire has so far not been located again.

Apparently, the natives of the North Salem area paid little attention to the archaeological sites in their midst, including Mystery Hill. This is not particularly surprising, since the hill is covered by dense woods, difficult to reach, and, except during the dry summer months, an impossible quagmire of mud and underbrush. Then, too, why should they have paid attention to what appeared to the naked eye as merely a shambles of helter-skelter stone slabs that sometimes looked like ruined houses and sometimes simply like heaps of stones? Thus, farmers of the surrounding countryside simply behaved in an eminently practical fashion—they carted off stones for use in building. This continued for centuries.

Jonathan Pattee, who occupied Mystery Hill between 1823 and 1848, was a French Huguenot farmer. During his lifetime, people of the area believed that he had built the strange structures on the hill to hold supplies, especially bootleg whiskey, and at one time he acquired the reputation of shielding runaway slaves. These impressions, however, were not factual at all. Pattee had most likely acquired the site because he liked the seclusion of the hill or perhaps because he found some romance in living in caves and semisecret underground shelters. He altered some of the structures very slightly to suit his needs, adding touches of his own here and there. He fixed up one of the shelters for his personal use and otherwise made himself at home amongst the ruins. Pattee was not a poor farmer, but a man of some means. Local records show that he was a trustee of the town and that at one time he even donated a building to be used as the town school house. There is nothing on record to show that Pattee built the structures on Mystery Hill.

Although there is no previous owner on record for the site, history records indicate that severe earthquakes occurred in the area in 1638 and again in 1759. These must have wrought considerable damage to the structures and may be blamed, in part, for their present condition. Since the area was open to one and all, stone robbers probably took considerable numbers of the slabs and smaller stones over the years. Pattee, in addition to making one of the ancient shelters into a kind of cave home away from home, built himself a house on the site between 1832 and 1835 and lived there until his death in 1848. He used the area as a quarry, having discovered the abundance of natural bedrock in the area. It may well be that the bedrock deposits of the hill induced Pattee to buy the site in the first place, just as they may have attracted the original settlers to the area.

Pattee's house burned down in 1857 while it was occupied by local Indians. The hill then became quasi-public domain and was used as a hideout by shady elements. Eventually, a second stone quarry was opened by builders from the towns of Lawrence and Andover, Massachusetts, who carted away much of the ancient material to be used in their operations. From 1870 to 1920, the hill fell into oblivion and was probably used again as a hideaway by people who had reasons to shun society. In 1906, the North Salem town historian wrote, "This hilltop is a wild but beautiful spot among rough boulders and soft pine, about which the most weird and fantastic tales may be woven."

Enter one William B. Goodwin, retired insurance executive and amateur archaeologist from Hartford, Connecticut. In his peregrinations around the New England countryside, Goodwin discovered Pattee's Caves. He bought the hill and the land around it in 1920 and decided to devote all of his energies to excavating what he felt was a major archaeological site. Unfortunately, Goodwin was not a trained archaeologist, and in his eagerness to discover artifacts and restore the site to what he considered to be its original status, he destroyed much valuable evidence.

Goodwin approached his task with a preconceived notion about the origins of the hill. Having studied the history of the Irish monks called the Culdees who had come to New England contemporaneously with the Vikings, Goodwin had decided that Mystery Hill was in fact the remains of an Irish monastery, and he dedicated all his efforts to proving this theory. For the next fourteen years, he spent considerable amounts of time and money excavating the hill. However, instead of using professional archaeologists with their delicate brush-and-trowel method, he relied on untrained local helpers. As a result, anything they uncovered that was not likely to prove Goodwin's theory of Greater Ireland was discarded, and boulders and stones were moved from where they were found into what Goodwin considered their "rightful" positions. Despite this, and despite the fact that in the 1920s carloads upon carloads of stones were carted off to the city of Lawrence, Massachusetts, to be used for building streets and sewers, enough of the original stones remained in place at Mystery Hill to tell the story of its origin.

Before Goodwin died in 1950, he put his beliefs into a book, published in 1946, entitled *The Ruins of Greater Ireland in New England*. Were there in fact bands of Irish monks at Mystery Hill? The editors of *Science Digest*, under the direction of William F. Dempewolff, took up the question in their book *Lost Cities and Forgotten Tribes*. They concluded: "Nothing was ever discovered to prove that Goodwin's monks ever had lived there; yet he clung to his theory until he died in 1950."

Author Charles Michael Boland (*They All Discovered America*) felt otherwise. He wrote that not only is the presence of Irish monks in North America documented in the Icelandic sagas and by artifacts discovered in various parts of the United States, but that the Irish monks had both the skill to cross the sea and the need to do so in order to escape the pillaging of the Norsemen, who had become the bane of their existence both in Ireland and later in the New World. Boland said that from Newfoundland, the monks sailed down the coast and eventually wound up at the Merrimack River. Up the river at what is now Haverhill, their river voyage was ended by the falls, so they took to land, following an ancient Indian trail that led them straight to Mystery Hill. Boland summarized, "In short, they had arrived at Pattee's Caves—the site of a Phoenician occupation more than a thousand years before. We have no way of knowing whether the peregrinating Irishmen found Pattee's Caves by accident or whether they learned about it from the Indians."

After Goodwin's death, nothing happened at the hill until 1955, when the Early Site Foundation, an association of amateur archaeologists, decided to excavate the hill. They commissioned Dr. Junius Bird, of the American Museum of Natural History, and Gary Vescelius, an archaeologist who had received his education at Yale, to do the actual work. Both men were familiar with the site when it had belonged to Goodwin. Vescelius sank ten test pits into the site, which yielded thousands of artifacts. However, after six weeks he and Bird concluded that there was no evidence at the site of anything but colonial occupation. Their report seemed to disprove Goodwin's theory of Greater Ireland. So convincing was it that the other members of the Early Site Foundation accepted the findings as the last word in the matter.

Only one man in the foundation, Frank Glynn, felt that the tests had been insufficient and that the mystery of the hill had not been penetrated. He continued to investigate the site on his own. Glynn, then president of the Connecticut Archaeological Society, discovered architectural parallels to a Bronze Age culture amongst the ruins of the hill.

Dismissing the ruins as "colonial" also did not sit well with a number of informed archaeologists, even though the hard-core establishment scientists refused to discuss the matter further. Anthropologist Sharon McKern commented on the ruins of Mystery Hill in her book *Exploring the Unknown*:

> At Poverty Point in northern Louisiana, vast terraces and strange earth hummocks are neatly arranged in concentric circles. No one knows who built them, or when, or why. In the Ohio and Mississippi valleys, giant effigy mounds, some containing tombs, ramble along the landscape to form in low relief the outlines of birds, beasts, reptiles, and man. These, too, are the work of a vanished race—one whose prehistoric purposes are lost in the shifting sands of time. But more mystifying still are the curious manmade caves of Mystery Hill. . . . No one knows who pried and levered the heavy granite slabs into place, or why the builders laboured to erect this strange stone village. Even the date of construction remains in dispute. After more than thirty years of investigation, archaeologists can agree on but a single point: Mystery Hill may forever defy explanation.

In 1956, Frank Glynn was joined by another archaeological enthusiast, Robert E. Stone. Of practical bent, Stone decided to invite the public to help excavate the site by contributing money when they visited it, and he therefore opened the site to tourists in 1958. At the same time, he hoped that the visitors, who would soon come in ever-increasing numbers, might also carry news of this extraordinary site to the outside world and stir up enough interest amongst powerful historical groups to help him uncover the rest of the ruins. Stone knew very well that much remained to be done. Large sections of the ruins had become invisible to the eye and were perhaps as much as eight or ten yards underground, entrenched in deep mud but capable of being excavated provided one had the means to finance a proper expedition.

Thus it was that on July 11, 1958, the governor of New Hampshire officially opened the site to the general public. The news media were invited, and Stone and his associates did everything in their power to call attention to what they considered the most important archaeological site in America. Accounts of the hill continued to appear in various books as the mystery attracted more researchers. By 1964, Stone and like-minded individuals had decided to charter the New England Antiquities Research Association (NEARA), whose avowed purpose was to solve the mystery of Mystery Hill and similar structures throughout New England.

The fact that Robert Stone, a private citizen, had to round up workers to delve into the true background of the site he owned, which if it were situated in Europe or Asia would be a national monument under the protection of governmental antiquities laws, speaks volumes about the common attitude among Americans toward their own history beyond that of a scant few hundred years ago. The history of baseball, to them, is considered much more important. Had Stone not acted as he did, the site and its precious artifacts might have been plowed under to make room for a motel or fast-food restaurant.

Of course, the voice of Robert Stone did not stand alone in the wilderness of ignorance and neglect: Salvatore Michael Trento, the director of the Middletown Archeological Research Center in New York and a graduate of Oxford, wrote about and displayed actual photographs of some amazing pre-Christian artifacts and inscribed stones in his excellent book *The Search for Lost America*. Lost, indeed!

This issue of pre-Christian artifacts is not, however, strictly a New England matter. There is, for example, the "troublesome" find of four intact Roman amphorae, or wine jars, and the broken pieces of some fifty more, found fifteen miles from Rio de Janeiro. As the *New York Times* (I am sure, reluctantly) wrote on October 10, 1982, a professional underwater explorer and archaeologist named Robert Marx found the Roman wine jars in what appeared to be the wreck of a Roman vessel that had obviously gotten off course—far off course. Dr. Harold E. Edgerton of the Massachusetts Institute of Technology, who worked with Robert Marx, attested to their authenticity and the circumstances of their discovery. "Rio Artifacts May Indicate Roman Visit," the *New York Times* headline ran. Today, I have yet to hear of a single attempt to further explore the Roman wreck.

The United States's good neighbor to the south, Mexico, has also discovered many authentic relics brought across the ocean by people from the Mediterranean. The Museo Antropología in Mexico City, for instance, has on view a stele (or stone plaque) depicting a male figure wearing Phoenician-style headgear. The figure is a very Semitic-looking person, presumably a priest, whose earring has a Star of David engraved upon it.

Another example of a pre-Columbian artifact found in the United States is the stone found at Bourne, Massachusetts, inscribed with the Phoenician words "Hanno of Carthage takes possession of this place." This was the same Hanno, member of a distinguished ruling family, who sailed successfully down the coast of West Africa in 525 B.C.

Naturally, some people, especially conventional scientists, are quick to label such stones as hoaxes. But why and to what purpose? No money has changed hands. No wonderful publicity has been the result. If anything, those who would let the world in on what they have found are heaped with scorn and ridicule.

All over Pennsylvania, Virginia, and even as far inland as Oklahoma, Phoenician inscriptions of unquestionable authenticity and age have been found—sometimes on carved stones, sometimes on natural boulders. Who can doubt that the Phoenician sailors, excellent navigators and shipbuilders that they were, could cross the Atlantic and, once they had landed, explore the territory inland? Why would they come only to the coast and not go further?

Further evidence is the fact that Mexico has Olmec statuary and carved heads whose features clearly resemble those of African people. The Phoenicians are known to have enslaved black people in Carthage's hinterland. They must have brought some of these unfortunates with them into the New World.

Photo 1. *Approaching Mystery Hill main site.*

Photo 2. *The Megaron.*

Photo 3. *Entrance to Oracle Chamber.*

Photo 4. *Entrance to Oracle Chamber speaking tube.*

Photo 5. *Oracle Chamber, altar, and entrance to drain.*

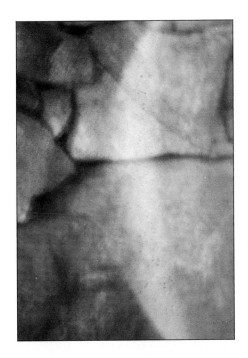

Photo 6. *Psychic impression inside Oracle Chamber.*

Photo 7. *Rear exit of Oracle Chamber.*

Photo 8. *Sacrificial Table, from below.*

Photo 9. *Psychic energy emanations at Sacrificial Table.*

Photo 10. *Nancy Abel psychometrizing Sacrificial Table, June 1975.*

Photo 11. *Unidentified structure, main site.*

Photo 12. *Large structure, not yet identified.*

Photo 13. *Large shrine.*

Photo 14. *Stone walls near main site.*

Photo 15. *Robert Stone examining radiocarbon dating reports, 1969.*

Photo 16. *Winter solstice monolith.*

Photo 17. *Equinox slab, now lying in wall.*

Photo 18. *The "seal stone."*

Photo 19. *Wall at distance from temple area.*

Photo 20. *Outer wall with monoliths.*

Photo 21. *Tomb of Lost Souls.*

Photo 22. *Close-up, Tomb of Lost Souls.*

Photo 23. *Astronomical monolith with human face.*

Photo 24. *Robert Stone and fellow archaeologist Osborn Stone.*

Photo 25. *Ingrid Beckman getting impressions at main site.*

Photo 26. *Main altar.*

Photo 27. *Ingrid Beckman examining the Megaron.*

Photo 28. *Boulder showing ship engraving.*

Photo 29. *Ethel Johnson Meyers getting psychic impressions from monolith.*

Photo 30. *Carving on boulder at main site.*

Photo 31. *Carving on boulder near "Indian Cliff."*

Photo 32. *Triangular stone in administration building.*

Photo 33. *Inscribed stone in administration building.*

Photo 34. *Walking toward the "Indian Cliff" area of the winter solstice monolith.*

NEARA GOES TO WORK ON MYSTERY HILL

With the establishment of NEARA, the New England Antiquities Research Association, a new name dawned over the ruins of North Salem: Mystery Hill. This title began to replace the previous one of Pattee's Caves.

Although Mystery Hill is by no means the only site in which the association is interested, it is the flagship, the association's pride and joy. When members of NEARA have uncovered other sites of a megalithic nature in New England, they are usually referred back to Mystery Hill to see if any relationship might exist. This does not mean the association is disinterested in other cultures or is concentrating solely on the Phoenician explorers and other ancient incursions into New England. They are intrigued when they discover any artifacts at all, pre-Columbian or post-Columbian. In its statement of intent, the association affirms that its purpose is to "add to existing knowledge of the prehistory and early history of New England and its surrounding areas, especially in relation to the unexplained stone structures, monoliths, and petroglyphs with which [its] area abounds."

Membership is open to sincere individuals, whether they are professional archaeologists or not. Members are expected to help in locating, measuring, and mapping sites; searching for and recording local traditions and legends pertaining to those sites; reading and researching archaeological books and articles to ferret out material bearing on the work of the association; and even assisting with clerical and administrative work relating to the sites discovered or under the control of the association. However, NEARA was not founded to be a free-for-all explorers' club—the memory of William Goodwin's enthusiastic but damaging method of excavating at Mystery Hill is still too recent. According to its statement of intent, "while NEARA encourages active field work in the way of locating and recording sites, it does not encourage unsupervised excavations."

NEARA has chosen for its symbol a primitive image of a human body, possibly female, with legs slightly spread, surrounded by a linear frame. Robert Stone explains the choice of this symbol and its relationship to Mystery Hill: "The symbol was adopted from a figure carved into a granite slab presently standing on top of Mineral Mountain, Shrewsbury, Massachusetts. It is said to have been found part way down the hill's north side, buried a foot and a half deep, by two men filling soil for a potato patch a quarter of a century ago. The stone itself is about three feet high, and the eighteen-inch carving was done in relief."

Above the carved figure, there is an arrow pointing to the left, and below it is a small circle. "The symbol is the only carving in relief thus far recorded in NEARA's files," Stone continues. "Another interesting feature is that the outline around the figure closely resembles the bell-shaped Sacrificial Table at Mystery Hill, located about one hundred miles away. Also, the circle below the figure is in the approximate position of where a vessel would sit if placed under the carved exit channel of the table." The area of Mineral Mountain was once a health resort due to the presence of mineral springs, which may have existed there for a long time.

In September 1967, work at Mystery Hill took another turn. Funds had been collected to permit a radiocarbon dating test of some of the materials found, and Geochrone Laboratories of Cambridge, Massachusetts, was entrusted with the task. The radiocarbon dating was done on a sample of pine stump. The analysis, dated September 18, 1967, appeared in full in the NEARA Newsletter. It stated: "We have determined an age of 260 plus or minus 90 C-14 years B.P., which would correspond to a calendar date of A.D. 1690." Technical director Harold W. Krueger then added, "I think we can establish at least that Pattee himself did not build the particular structure which is penetrated by the roots of the white pine stump. It is still not clear, however, whether these ruins could be colonial, but considerably older than Pattee."

The popular assumption that the ruins were simply the remains of structures built by farmer Pattee (which some professional archaeologists were giving out as an explanation for their refusal to deal further with Mystery Hill) was now disproved. It is also significant that NEARA members did not insist upon a particular point of view for their explanation of the ruins at Mystery Hill, as Goodwin had done in seeking proof of his theory that Irish monks had built it. NEARA was only interested in discovering the facts about the hill, whatever those facts might be. At that early stage, especially, NEARA members had not yet settled on any particular point of view. In the December 1967 NEARA *Newsletter*, Frank Glynn reported on excavations at Mystery Hill in the years 1966 and 1967:

> Our goal proved easier to state than to accomplish. It was to obtain charcoal samples capable of radiocarbon-14 dating from a context which could reasonably be shown to be related to the first human occupation. Since the most notable site features lie roughly along a line between the northern end of the Y-cave and the southern area "improved" by Jonathan Pattee as a homestead, we confined our searches to that section, riddled though it is by the prior digging of Pattee, Goodwin, Early Site Foundation, and others.

They started with a drain running eastward from the cellar of what used to be called Pattee's barn, where no previous excavation showed. The archaeologists felt that the deepest materials at the lower end of the drain would date the first occupation of the cellar area. They dug an intercepter trench and, as luck would have it, exposed the drain's disposal field: fair-sized blocks of quarried granite deeply imbedded in undisturbed subsoil. The method used by the team of archaeologists was ingenious indeed. Glynn stated:

> A small radio transmitter was mounted ahead of a plumber's snake and worked down the drain, while a radio receiver on top of the mound, seven to eight feet overhead, permitted precise staking of the drain's course. The final seven feet of the drain were then exposed and the deepest three inches of the twelve to fifteen inches of the fill in the drain were removed for examination.

Samples of this area were then submitted to radiocarbon dating, resulting in the dates A.D. 1810 and A.D. 1550. This finding of the laboratory appeared indecisive to the archaeologists, so they returned to the site for further investigations of the deepest layers of the same drain. Glynn commented:

> The work was done by James Whittall, aided by Marjorie Chandler and Barbara Edfords. The sump-pit area was reexcavated, yielding two fragments of a primitive pottery. . . . a hitherto undisturbed portion

of the drain was excavated. . . . unfortunately, the charcoal content was insufficient for a determination.

Again, the intrepid explorers returned to the site. This time, the samples examined yielded the date A.D. 1690. Glynn continued:

Digging continued downwards in a column averaging thirty-plus inches in depth. At a point three to six inches above bedrock an old occupation surface was met. . . . two samples were taken for radiocarbon testing. . . . The laboratory results are not known. The site is not yet "dated." But we have isolated, roughly in the middle of the complex, the old land surface in use when the first major human activity— granite quarrying—was being carried out.

James P. Whittall, Jr., chief archaeologist for NEARA, added his own report to that of Glynn.

The results of this excavation were helpful and shed new light on the hill's history. The discovery of stone tools that are very similar to those found in Europe, classed as Neolithic, is certainly a new angle to consider in relation to Mystery Hill. . . . The question of Neolithic tools is particularly interesting because up to this time they have not been considered. . . . The tools fall into three categories: (1) two-handed shovels, (2) one-handed scrapers, and (3) stone picks or choppers of various sizes. These all show various degrees of shaping by man, and their numbers and consistencies rule out their being works of nature. They have strong similarity to Neolithic tools of Europe, some being identical in appearance to those found in the ditches at Stonehenge, which can be seen at the museum at Salisbury, England.

In the midst of renewed activities at Mystery Hill, Frank Glynn, its archaeological pioneer, died on August 16, 1968. Continuance of the excavations now fell to James Whittall and Robert Stone. The results of the 1968 excavations were reported by Whittall in the *Newsletter* of March 1969:

Most of the work performed was in the area just south of the Megaron, or Pattee cellar hole. In a test trench, Frank Glynn in 1958 recovered some granular, impressed potsherds here. A fairly large area was excavated this time, but beyond the numerous expected colonial artifacts, results were lean. However, we did recover some interesting potsherds.

The pottery sherds were displayed in the *Newsletter* with the remark that they were "similar to prehistoric Iberian impressed ware in Spain and Portugal." Whittall continued his report:

One other artifact was of an unusual character: a small piece of hard leather, with fragmentary painted design, which appeared in Level C, forty-three inches below the surface duff. These artifacts are under further investigation. Also recovered were more stone shovels and picks as well as scrapers similar to those previously noted. . . . Also of interest were some quartz crystals which appeared to have been worked in an attempt to utilize them in some manner, perhaps as projectile points.

By the time the June 1969 *Newsletter* appeared, there was exciting news from Mystery Hill. On May 17, 1969, about twenty-five members and guests of the association had gathered to do some research in the area. Despite the fact that it was a particularly hot day, they worked feverishly. Under the direction of chief archaeologist James Whittall, they extracted tiny bits of charcoal from a level of soil twenty-four inches down and two inches above bedrock. Eventually, enough material was extricated to fill two small jars, and this sample was immediately rushed to the Geochrone Laboratories in Cambridge, Massachusetts, as before.

The material was taken from the area where in 1967 a decayed piece of pine rock had been found within the walls and had yielded an A.D. 1690 carbon test date. This time, however, the archaeologists hit "pay dirt." In his report to the association, the director of the laboratory stated that the sample was almost three thousand years old. A jubilant Robert Stone declared, "This history-making breakthrough will revolutionize all previous concepts of American prehistory. . . . [the dating] has for thirty years eluded all investigators of this strange complex of megalithic constructions."

As if this precedent-setting discovery were not enough to make this a banner day in the history of NEARA, William Nisbet, one of the amateur archaeologists, uncovered a triangular stone slab, fourteen by sixteen inches across and about two and a half inches thick, with an incised groove around the edges on one side and several deeply cut markings similar to those found on Neolithic pottery on the island of Malta. The slab was discovered in a "ruined chamber" near the site where the carbon dating sample had been taken.

Mystery Hill was now firmly established as a site that had been in existence since as long ago as 1000 B.C. In view of this and previous discoveries of pottery and stone tools showing links with late Neolithic and Bronze Age megalithic cultures of the Mediterranean area, "a consistent picture of the site's probable origin started to emerge," Stone declared.

Meanwhile, excavations continued. In his December 1969 report to the membership, James Whittall was able to report that further digging had been concluded on the north side of the Megaron area, in the center of the site, and that work had also continued at the so-called Watch House. Amongst items uncovered there was a pig's tooth and an excellent stone tool, eleven inches long. By now, the archaeologists working on the site knew that they had to cope with several layers of occupation, dating back at least to the pre-Christian period and ending with the ownership of Jonathan Pattee. They were careful to separate the various artifacts found at the site and to establish, as much as possible, the different periods of human occupation.

Toward the end of August 1969, the archaeologists decided to investigate a small bog near the temple site. Stone wrote in the fall/winter *Newsletter*, "The evidence of the area seems to indicate that the material for making pottery was prepared here. Quartz spallings, heavily fire burned, were found in conjunction with quartz grit, as well as a small hand hammer for reducing the fired quartz to a grit filler. Numerous hand scrapers as well as stone tools for shaping pots were uncovered."

On April 3, 1970, Mystery Hill got yet another boost. The NBC television program "The Unknown," presented by Encyclopaedia Britannica, featured a segment devoted to Mystery Hill. Robert Stone, James Whittall, and Dr. Cyrus Gordon all spoke on the subject of Mystery Hill, a "3,000-year-old American outpost of the West European Bronze Age megalithic culture."

The March 1970 *Newsletter* also carried an article by Robert Stone concerning a strange well found at Mystery Hill—the so-called Upper Well, which was first excavated in the summer of 1961. At that time, a great deal of debris, rock dirt, and accumulated junk was removed from about the twelve-foot level to the eighteen-foot level. During that dig, a large number of quartz crystal clusters of various sizes were found mixed in with the debris. Many of them are now on display in the administration building at Mystery Hill.

"Before, and particularly after, the 1961 dig," Stone explained, "there were persistent rumors and stories concerning the well, ranging all the way from it being an underground tomb, a mine shaft, a sacrificial well, a religious well, or an ancient wishing well into which the quartz crystals were thrown. It was hoped that the 1963 dig would finally determine which of the rumors and stories were true." Stone himself descended into the well on a makeshift ladder with a safety rope attached to his waist. Many crystals were taken out of the well from layers that were vertical, not horizontal. This proved that the crystals were coming from a natural joint or fault in the bedrock.

Eventually, the bottom of the well was reached, twenty-two feet down. Stone commented:

> Who built the well is still anyone's guess. The stone wall at the bottom proves that the shaft was built over or partially in a natural fault in bedrock. . . . In conclusion, while no man-made artifacts were found during this excavation, at least one of the past stories has finally been answered. The well is certainly not the entrance to a burial tomb. But is it a well? Is is the beginning of a mine shaft? Who built it and when?

Almost in answer to Stone's 1970 questions, the *Newsletter* reported on a symposium of the Society for Early Historic Archaeology during which Dr. Ross T. Christensen spoke of the evidence for a megalithic origin of Mystery Hill.

> It looks as if the strange, rough-hewn structures of Mystery Hill and elsewhere in New England and New York State are about to be identified in terms of time period and point of origin, and the evidence so far argues in favour of a trans-Atlantic crossing. But apparently, those who came here were not Indian hunters, Yankee farmers, Irish monks, nor Phoenician mariners; they were a nameless people of the late Bronze Age of the western Mediterranean area, perhaps from Portugal.

In November 1970, the New Hampshire historical commission set up an official marker en route to Mystery Hill, reading:

> Four miles east on Route 3 is a privately owned complex of strange stone structures bearing similarities to early stonework found in western Europe. They suggest an ancient culture may have existed here more than 2,000 years ago. Sometimes called "America's Stonehenge," these intriguing chambers hold a fascinating story and could be remnants of pre-Viking or even Phoenician civilization.

About that time, the archaeologists exploring Mystery Hill turned their attention away from the buildings themselves and toward the wider horizons of the site. Here, boulders and man-made markers dot the landscape, indicating some sort of astronomical purpose for the entire site. Keeping in mind similar observatories elsewhere, especially Stonehenge, the members of NEARA set out to investigate all those "suspicious" stones within a two-mile radius of the principal site itself.

In the June 1971 *Newsletter*, Warren R. Martel, Jr., reported on astronomical alignment research at Mystery Hill in some detail. Robert Stone had already been in touch with Gerald Hawkins, author of *Stonehenge Decoded*, several years prior, in order to sound out the British expert concerning parallels between Stonehenge and Mystery Hill. Stone had felt that several prominent monoliths, when viewed from the altar stone, would line up with one or another of the major astronomical events. However, sufficient material could not be sent to Hawkins to allow him to come to any definite conclusions at that time.

Since 1971, a great deal about the monoliths has been discovered, and the alignments have been very carefully charted, so the usage of Mystery Hill as an astronomical observatory is no longer in doubt. In continuing his research as astronomical alignments coordinator, Warren Martel reminded his fellow archaeologists not to limit themselves to viewing the monoliths from the Sacrificial Table only, but to consider the possibility that the monoliths may have to be viewed from each other's perspectives.

Four elements must be considered when studying the usage of the monoliths: (1) the exact location of each monoliths, (2) the elevation of the horizons, (3) the elevation of each monolith, and (4) the azimuth of the major astronomical events. Only by having exact data on all four points can one come to any accurate conclusions.

While these studies were continuing, a new radiocarbon dating indicated an even greater antiquity for Mystery Hill. Based on the growth rings of the long-lived bristlecone pine trees of California, this radiocarbon dating of a charcoal sample obtained by James Whittall in June 1971 yielded a date of 1525 B.C., with an error range of plus or minus two hundred years. Thus, there is now an inhabitation date for the site of 1735 to 1315 B.C. The corrected median date of 1525 B.C. would be contemporary with the final development phase of Stonehenge and the Wessex culture of England. The charcoal samples were taken from levels two to four inches above bedrock, suggesting that they reflected a period at or shortly after the actual construction of the site.

About the same time, one of the pottery sherds found at the site was submitted for analysis to Florence Whitmore of the Boston Museum of Fine Arts research department. The result of a complicated x-ray process was surprising: the material used in making the pottery sherd was a common clay that contained traces of quartz and feldspar of Mediterranean or Near Eastern provenance.

While further studies at Mystery Hill continued unabated, the matter of the missing stones came to the attention of archaeologist Charles J. Lemay, who decided to search for some of these stones in the surrounding countryside and towns. In particular, Robert Stone brought his attention to two stones in a house in nearby Derry that were suspected of having originally come from Mystery Hill. The house was located on Frost Road and in 1972, when the investigation was undertaken, was occupied by Jean Lebesque and his family. It was originally erected by a Belgian-French immigrant, Joseph G. Dergis. The two stones in question were embedded in the house's walls on either side of a window. What was remarkable about the stones, other than their apparent great antiquity, was the fact that each had a human face engraved on it. According to NEARA, Lemay reported:

> I examined the faces carefully and found that the one on the right side of the window was carved in deep relief and consisted primarily of a smoky-white, semitranslucent quartz and white feldspar with some small garnet crystals interspersed. The face on the left side of the window was in very low relief and consisted of common granite. The features on both faces were similar, but those of the face on the right were less distinct: an outline of all but the top of the head, plus mouth, eyes, and the nose. The face on the left had two indentations for nostril holes and a subtle flaring of the lip. In addition, mortared into the eyeholes were two leather shoe buttons, now in my possession. Once the buttons were removed, they revealed two round holes about three-eighths of an inch deep, very smooth and rounded at the bottom.

Lemay made plaster casts of the faces and submitted them to the Peabody Museum at Harvard. Katherine Edsall, whose field was Indian pottery, "thought that they were impressions of a white man's work." After much further investigation and talking to various people who knew the previous owners of the house, Lemay came to the conclusion that the first of the two stone faces

cannot be attributed to any culture group known to have inhabited the

New England area. The piece is unique in its material and in its design, as far as I have been able to ascertain, and its association with Mystery Hill can neither be substantiated nor disproved unless similar examples are found in context and not in a twentieth-century wall.

With their broadness and their wide-set eyes, similar to eyes seen in pre-Hellenic Greece, the two faces, especially the one on the left, seem to me to have distinct parallels with ancient masks uncovered at Mycenae.

Meanwhile, excavations at Mystery Hill continued. In July 1972, the upper Processional Path, a double-stone-walled road on top of the hill leading into the woods in a northwesterly direction, was selected for excavation. At the site chosen, it appeared that a ten-foot section of the wall had at one time been deliberately removed and relaid at right angles across the path.

The purpose of the new excavation was to determine the nature of the missing section of stone wall and when it had been torn out. As the excavation proceeded, it became apparent that the base of the wall was still present. "A one-by-two-foot cut was made into the subsoil along the base of the wall on the inside," reported Edward J. Lenik in the *Newsletter* of December 1972.

> At this point the subsoil is light brown in colour and fine in texture. Several artifacts were removed from this test cut. A clearly recognizable hammer stone was found in this soil beneath the stone wall. This hammer stone showed clear evidence of usage, as one end was battered and a section of its side was rubbed smooth from handling. Two stone chips of the same material as the hammer stone were also recovered. One of these fits onto the battered end of the hammer stone and was obviously knocked off while it was being used.

In January 1973, NEARA's membership chairperson, Marjorie Kling, arranged for an exhibit at the Hillside Book Library in New Hyde Park, New York, to draw attention to America's lost prehistory and early history. Her opening remarks included recent news concerning astronomical alignments at Mystery Hill:

> One such alignment that appears to exist there involves the monolith referred to as the Winter Solstice Monument. It has been found that the winter solstice sun sets directly on this stone when viewed from the center of the Mystery Hill complex. Although this monolith is now separated from the rest of the complex by trees and brush, we believe

this was not the case at the time it was erected; rather, we feel, there was just a bare expanse of rock permitting an unobstructed view of it from the center of the site [see photo 16].

Pointing to one of the showcases of the exhibit, Mrs. Kling continued:

This is a drawing of one of the two carved stones found in the ruined chamber near the excavations. Note the similarity in the type of design here to that found in Malta, and also compare it with the design found carved on stone at the Raymond, New Hampshire, stone circle site.

In another exhibit area, Mrs. Kling had arranged a pen-and-ink transcription of tracings made in 1968 by Gertrude Johnson, a NEARA volunteer. The tracings were of an inscribed stone found at Mystery Hill in September of the previous year.

Some months later, a progress report came from the pen of Osborn Stone, a research consultant to the site. In the winter 1973 *Newsletter*, he stated:

Work was started in the spring by clearing trees and brush surrounding the main site. . . . During the search for fallen indicator monoliths, three pieces of sedimentary stones were found in the east wall of the Processional Path north of the site. One stone was worked and has the shape of a spade. . . . Other fallen indicator monoliths found throughout the wall surrounding the site need to be accurately aligned. Two of the largest are east of the site, running north from near the Watch House. Immediately west of the site are several walls yet to be thoroughly studied that contain large indicator monoliths, some fallen and some still standing. The final item of interest in this report is the sighting point for the winter solstice stone. One hundred feet east of this stone is a crescent-shaped wall that has been broken through. Wide sections of the wall appear to be observation points. Even more important is the fact that this monolith, when viewed from any position immediately behind the crescent-shaped wall, appears like a gun sight on the horizon with only the small projection on the top of the monolith appearing above the horizon.

In 1974, NEARA celebrated its tenth anniversary. Much had changed in ten years. Regular volunteer guides were now available during the summer months to take the considerable numbers of tourists around the site. Also, newspaper and magazine coverage was on the increase, and the resulting publicity was at least sufficient to keep the site financially stable. However, the income was not enough to undertake new excavations of any magnitude or to remove trees from the remainder of the hill. Robert Stone and his hard-working associates were still the main driving force behind Mystery Hill, and the great powerhouses of establishment archaeology in America were still to be convinced that ancient peoples from across the sea had built Mystery Hill. Instead of arguing about this theory, most traditional archaeological societies simply ignored it, hoping perhaps that it would go away in time. However, Mystery Hill did not go away, and more and more reputable scientists, such as Cyrus Gordon, came over to the side of those who believed that it was built by some very ancient mariners.

Among those who wrote about Mystery Hill prior to my own investigations was Sharon McKern. She took it for granted that Irish monks had not built the hill, but was impressed with the carbon dating evidence that positioned Mystery Hill nearly three thousand years in the past. In *Exploring the Unknown*, she, too, marveled at the lack of interest on the part of establishment archaeologists.

> There has been no rush of archaeologists to support the astonishing antiquity now assigned to the structures at Mystery Hill. But a few noted scholars have lent cautious support. Cyrus Gordon, professor of Mediterranean studies at Brandeis University, thinks it possible that about 1500 B.C. the men or the people who built Stonehenge reached the New World to construct the cell-like structures and erect a grooved table at Mystery Hill.

McKern speculated that "no matter how old the megaliths, they still must have been known to colonial inhabitants of New Hampshire. Yet there is no mention of it in colonial records; and no local legends, passed from generation to generation, survived to spread light on their origins." She then added a rather tantalizing suggestion: "Could the stone structures on Mystery Hill have served for occult practices in colonial times? They might have provided an appropriate setting for rites practiced by underground survivors of the Salem witch cult."

In a somewhat superficial and slanted survey of Mystery Hill in a magazine article in *Science Digest* entitled "Lost Cities and Forgotten Tribes" (adapted from the book), William F. Dempewolff brought together some of the negative views expressed by a variety of professional visitors to the hill.

Of the archaeologists who have made contact with Mystery Hill, most are unconvinced that there is any mystery at all. Dr. [Junius] Bird, for example, has not returned since his excavation in 1955 and doesn't feel any urge to do so. . . . According to [Gary] Vescelius, the mysterious buildings were used for storage purposes, the Oracle Chamber in particular for holding cider barrels, with the table serving as the base for a cider press. . . . More recently involved are Glyn Daniel, an expert in European archaeology and editor of the British archaeological magazine *Antiquity*, and Dr. Stephen Williams, an expert in North American archaeology and director of Harvard's Peabody Museum. Both went to New Hampshire after the 1971 dating was publicized— Williams out of professional curiosity and Daniel as part of a BBC film crew. . . . Daniel was unimpressed by what he saw and says as much in an editorial. . . . Dr. Williams' opinion was: "It's a very good Colonial construction." . . . During the same interview he also admitted that no one from Harvard had been to the site in over twenty years.

However, Dempewolff also presented the other side of the coin:

Not everyone in the academic community opposes NEARA. One sympathizer is Professor Ross T. Christensen of the Department of Anthropology and Archaeology of Brigham Young University, who believes the structures were plainly not built by New England Indians or their ancestors of any known variety. They clearly do not fit into the pattern of prehistoric cultural development usually assigned to the eastern woodlands area by professional archaeologists. Another is Cyrus Gordon, professor of Mediterranean studies at Brandeis University, who made news with the pronouncement that a small inscribed stone found in a burial mound in Tennessee in 1885 was evidence that Semites had landed in America a thousand years before Columbus. Gordon concludes that Mystery Hill is "definitely pre-Columbian, mainly due to the use of megaliths at the site."

On August 8, 1959, the austere *Saturday Evening Post* saw fit to commission an article on Mystery Hill by Evan Hill. The article was an honest attempt to shed light on "the strange secret of the New Hampshire hillside." At the time, Malcolm Pearson was the owner of the hill. Hill pointed out that the grotto known as the Tomb of Lost Souls at Mystery Hill bore a startling resemblance to ancient stone chapels on the island of Malta (see photos 21 and 22). Hill interviewed Roscoe A. Whitney, the man whom William Goodwin had hired to excavate the hill for him. "I measured every wall and every ramp and every building in that site,"

Whitney said, "and I found no place where the measurements were in feet or yards or inches. Whoever built that place either didn't give a damn about standard linear measure, or he didn't know it existed." Reporting on the work done by Frank Glynn, Hill said:

> Glynn has found more than a dozen architectural similarities with the 3,500-year-old Bronze Age civilization at Malta. Besides the oracle tube and sacrificial stone, he has noted stone seats and niches, which at Malta stored the bones and horns of sacrificed animals. The cells along North Salem's 106-foot ramp are similar to Malta's chapels. Like Whitney, Glynn found no standard linear measurements. He did discover a common scale in cubits, an ancient yardstick used by the Egyptians.

In 1963, the Anthropological Journal of Canada published an article by Andrew E. Rothovius, long connected with NEARA. The article stated that Mystery Hill, at a 245-foot elevation, had "its long axis running northwest-southeast" and is exactly twenty-five miles west of the Atlantic Ocean. It is

> on the east side of a shallow valley down which the Spicket River runs a few miles to the Merrimack estuary. Between 1730 and 1750, white settlements spread into the valley from two directions: southward from the centre of Scottish-Irish Presbyterian colonization (1721) at Derry, and northwestward from Methuen and Haverhill in Massachusetts. . . . By 1800 there were only five or six dwellings, two of them taverns on a road that had been laid out toward Haverhill. All were to the northeast of Pattee's Hill. Between the hill and the immediate valley bottom, the land remained uncultivated. The valley border on the east has almost the character of an escarpment, a precipitous cliff nearly two hundred feet in height forming the west side of Pattee's Hill. The cliff, although fifteen hundred feet west of the group of structures, may be an integral part of the site, since it has several arcades, galleries, and overhangs, many of which show signs of having been modified from naturally eroded cavities by the hand of man. Markings on the rock faces do not seem to have been made by modern metal tools.

The September 1967 issue of New England Homestead included an article entitled "New England's Greatest Mystery." In this article, Martha Wheeler Heilmann compared the artifacts of Mystery Hill with similar ones found elsewhere:

> More recently, the similarity between Mystery Hill and England's Stonehenge has been the subject of study. . . . Similarities of construc-

tion are obvious, but a further similarity to Stonehenge has been noted. Just as the English ruins have stones placed in several concentric circles, it has been discovered that some forty-six individual stones (menhirs) are located around the perimeter of Pattee's Caves at some little distance from the main colony. A curious aspect is that, in at least some instances, the stone walls surrounding the settlement are notched for the alignment of the menhirs, not unlike the sight of a gun. Have these stones, like those at Stonehenge, an astronomical significance? If this can be proved, it could be the first real breakthrough in establishing both the age and the origin of New Hampshire's mysterious megaliths.

Heilmann then reported that NEARA was compiling measurements and other data on the forty-six outlying individual stones and that the data would be turned over and fed into computers in an attempt to determine whether Mystery Hill might actually have been an ancient observatory. She pointed out that the so-called Tomb of Lost Souls was similar to dolmens found in Malta that served the ritual purpose of confining otherwise harmful spirits of the dead by forcing them into dead-end chambers connected to each other.

Cycles, a magazine published by the Foundation for the Study of Cycles, ran an article by Sandy Stevens entitled "Stones Alien in Time" in its February 1969 issue. Stevens stated, "The Megaron House, the only structure large enough to have been used as a dwelling place . . . bears a striking resemblance to the square-shaped structures which are common to the Aegean or Mycenaean in Greek history." He went on to note that "elaborate drainage systems run throughout all the structures in the main complex, and some of them may have been underground connecting passages, although they are shallow."

Stevens then quoted Frank Glynn concerning the carving of a deer in one of the caves, which Glynn compared to a carving found in a cave on the island of Malta:

> Many scholars believe the stone structures were part of an ancient religious shrine, and one professor, Dr. Charles H. Hapgood, of Keene Teachers College, New Hampshire, has a theory that the shrine was built by the Phoenicians more than thirty-five hundred years ago.

United Press International, under the dateline February 7, 1969, ran the headline, "West European Culture Here in 1000 B.C.?" The article stated:

Many archaeologists have felt that Phoenicians and other Bronze Age sea adventurers may have crossed the Atlantic, using the prevailing winds and currents, which would sweep them southwesterly, then up the American east coast. To return to western Europe, the seafarers would only have to ride the same circle of currents and winds going northeast, then down to Iberia and the Mediterranean.

In the 1970s, *Argosy* magazine, always on the lookout for unusual reports, published an illustrated article entitled "America's Prehistoric Riddle," by Arthur Goldsmith. After examining all the evidence at Mystery Hill and weighing the pros and cons of its antiquity, Goldsmith discussed the Sacrificial Table, probably the most controversial object at the site.

> What kind of liquid dripped from the stone? Blood from a sacrifice, possibly human? Animal sacrifices certainly seem to be a possibility, as a small stone pen big enough to hold a couple of goats, lambs, or pigs lies close to the table. However, skeptics have denied that there is any sacrificial purpose for this curious stone and say it's only a cider press. If so, this must have been the strangest cider mill in all New England. An artificially constructed ramp hooks up to a retaining wall directly in front of the table. Facing toward the rising sun, it is large enough to hold a sizable group of spectators, possibly worshippers. Even more curious is the speaking tube, a small tunnel leading back to several feet of rock into a large T-chamber directly behind the table. You can't see the opening from above. In fact, you must kneel down or crawl under the table to detect it. But a person inside the chamber can speak into the tube and project his voice to the outside. I stood on the ramp and heard Casey, my young guide, do just that. The effect is weird and convincing: a voice apparently emerging from deep underground, the voice of an oracle, perhaps, or a god to whom a sacrifice has been made. Similar oracle tubes have been found in ancient sites in Malta and other European locations, but I've never heard of one being used as part of cider operations.

This reference was, of course, an ironic comment upon the oft-heard "explanation" by professional archaeologists that the Sacrificial Table was nothing more than a New England cider press.

New Hampshire Echoes, a magazine published in Concord, carried an article entitled "The Mystery at Mystery Hill" in fall 1973. Accompanied by superb color photographs, the mood of the article by Joyce Zinn was one of sober reflection upon the purpose of Mystery Hill. Amongst the photographs was one taken on December 21, 1970, showing the winter solstice monolith and the setting sun exactly in line with the center of the site, which is where the Sacrificial Table is located.

The following year, the magazine of the Merrimack Valley Region Association published an account of Mystery Hill that was copied from Zinn's article, giving the site even wider exposure in the area. As a result of this, the December 1974 *New Hampshire Reader* devoted a special section to Mystery Hill. This elaborate article by Mark Feldman was probably one of the best pieces of writing to emerge on the subject. "Of all the stone structures, however, there is one site which is so baffling and mysterious," Feldman wrote, "yet so prominent in its scope that future historians may be required to completely rewrite the ancient history of North America."

Feldman suggested that both Stonehenge and Mystery Hill were constructed around 1700 B.C. He pointed out the importance of recent astronomical surveys, especially those involving the alignment of the many stones around the central complex. Swaths were cut through the trees in order to see how the stones would link up with the horizon. Notes were taken on how far above or below the horizon the top of each stone appeared to be. All the stones studied lined up within five degrees of their respective horizons. Cutting down the trees in order to create the corridors was not an easy task.

Osborn Stone, Robert Stone's cousin, took a somewhat different approach in 1973 when he concentrated his efforts on the exact location of the north stone in relation to the pole star, Polaris. A swath was cut in the trees to connect the stone with the Sacrificial Table. This disclosed that the monolith was located at true north from the Sacrificial Table. However, much further research and new plottings were needed in order to ascertain the exact nature of the observatory.

Since some funds had become available to the association, Osborn Stone engaged the surveying firm of Beverly Pearson Associates of Derry, New Hampshire, to conduct a new astronomical survey. Using a theodolite, a surveyor's tool to measure angles and distances, the Pearson company was able to plot the polar star much more accurately than the archaeologists had been able to do. Data obtained from these surveys were fed into computers to help form an accurate picture of the site and its astronomical purposes.

Charles Berlitz, author of the best-selling book *The Bermuda Triangle*, also commented on Mystery Hill. In *Mysteries from Forgotten Worlds,* he examined the archaeological evidence from ancient civilizations as it pertains to the Americas. "The United States, long regarded archaeologically as a sort of parvenu among nations, may yet reserve some surprises for the studies of prehistory," he declared. He gave the age of Mystery Hill as 2,790 years. He then went on to say that

> no identifiable writing has yet been translated from Mystery Hill, although letters and symbols have been found which seem to resemble Phoenician or a similar alphabet. Other apparently Phoenician letters were found in Mechanicsburg, Pennsylvania, starting in 1948, when about a thousand grooved stones were found, marked not with inscriptions but with single Phoenician letters.

Figure 4. *Inscription in stone in the Megaron. Archaic letters TNQE possibly stand for "Ton ke," which may be an incantation.*

Mystery Hill still stands quietly in New Hampshire, inviting visitors to come and marvel at its ruins. Nobody much talks about Indians at Mystery Hill anymore, and no Indian tribe has come forward to lay claim to it. Why would they? No one has ever heard of ancient Indians, ingenious though they were, building sophisticated sacrificial tables of stone with hidden speaking tubes leading to a building some distance away. And how many Indians of the past knew the Celtiberian or Phoenician alphabet?

Despite brave men like Robert Stone, Salvatore Michael Trento, and Barry Fell, the American public and the entrenched scientific community seem to prefer to let sleeping mysteries lie.

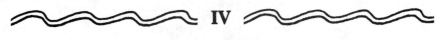
Ingrid Beckman at Mystery Hill

June 12, 1974, was a bright, clear day, ideally suited for an expedition of the kind Ingrid Beckman and I had undertaken at infrequent intervals during the preceding three years. An artist by profession, Ingrid had also developed her psychic abilities to the point of professional qualifications. Yet she had not ventured forth into the great world of psychic competition, but had simply been working closely with me to develop her skills. Ingrid had no spiritualistic affiliations or other involvements with metaphysics. Rather, she was a rational, cautious individual who required proof before she would accept any unusual data.

Ingrid had worked with me successfully in a number of haunted houses. Recently, she and I had been involved in a very confidential criminal investigation, for which we were summoned to the Midwest. Her ability lay primarily in the area of psychometry and clairvoyance, although I had seen her in a semitrance when the thoughts and feelings of an unseen entity were expressed through her. She had not yet achieved a full-trance state such as that experienced by Ethel Johnson Meyers; however, such abilities take many years to develop.

During our short flight to New Hampshire, I had deliberately steered my conversation with Ingrid away from Mystery Hill. Upon our arrival, Ingrid and I were greeted by Dorothy Stone, Sally Johansen, secretary of NEARA, and Osborn Stone, the man who had been so active in researching the alignments of the monoliths around the principal site. Carrying only the most necessary equipment, we began the steep ascent of Mystery Hill. As soon as we arrived at the ruins complex, Ingrid squinted at me in the peculiar way I had come to recognize as a sure sign that she was getting psychic impressions from her surroundings. I waited patiently until she had something to say.

"My first impression was that this was an outdoor place," said Ingrid. "Always outdoors, never enclosed in any way—almost an arena with different levels, radiating outward in concentric circles. It was on the highest spot they could find, and I believe they came to the highest spot because they felt they were closer to the gods. They felt they were cleaner spiritually. I had the impression as I walked by some of these little alcoves that during the initiations, especially at night, the initiates would wait in the alcoves until it was their time to come out. They were hidden until they were brought to the attention of the gods, so to speak."

"Who were the people who built it?" I asked, but Ingrid hadn't quite gotten her bearings yet and asked for more time. However, she did feel that pagans from a very early era had constructed the site.

When we stood by the main altar, Ingrid felt that we were at the very center of the complex. There were three distinctive cuts in the altar, and I pointed them out to Ingrid, asking her what she thought of them (see photo 26). She said, "I think they are symbolic. At first I thought they might have been used in building the site, but I feel they represent three elements or qualities or something of that nature."

Ingrid touched the indentations in the rock. "I want to say something about Greece—that this civilization sprang from ancient Greece, and the three elements have something to do with the gods. There is something pre-Hellenic, and I get a name like Mesma. It's very, very ancient Greece."

We walked over to a passage, and Ingrid touched one of the stone slabs standing next to it. "I think this was a passageway for young boys, for part of their ritual," she said. "Young boys were involved in this ritual—not as a sacrifice but as a peace offering to the gods, to show good faith. I think these children were used pretty much in the same way we use children today in weddings, as servants, or to offer peace offerings. I think the children were sent through here during the high rituals, and they may have carried gifts to the altar. I sense that they went right through here where we are standing, and that this was symbolic of being born— this going through a small opening. From here, they popped out into the main area. I think the entire complex was laid out to symbolize human development, indicating a whole civilization as well as even the smallest part of it. It was like the birth of a child relating to the gods. All this I sense here."

We entered a wide, Y-shaped subterranean chamber. Ingrid touched a wall. "I think this area was used for offerings, and there may have been ashes here at times. They were human ashes, not left here to be buried, but put here for a certain time for acceptance by the gods. When a high person in the community died, I think there was a ceremony, and his ashes were brought here. It was hoped that they would be received by the gods, by leaving them here for several days."

I asked Ingrid if she was able to get the names of the gods. "I'm getting the words *Pan* and *Mesme—Mesme* or *Mesma*," she responded. I see mourners coming here and leaving a clay jar or a vase with ashes in it. There is a very large ritual beforehand, and then the jar is left for several days."

"Is this part of a larger building above ground, or is this part we are standing in all there is?" I asked.

"This is part of a larger building; this small alcove is used strictly for the purpose I mentioned. I think every alcove here is used for different purposes. They are like little rooms."

"Why do you think this is in the shape of a *Y*?"

"I think the letter *Y* stands for the three major gods, in addition to which they have the gods of the north, south, east, and west."

I asked if she could pinpoint the names of these specific gods. "I'm getting Pan and Mesma again, and Titan," she said. "They rule different areas of their civilization."

Figure 5a. *Ingrid Beckman's symbols for Jupiter, Mars, and Venus.*

Later, while we were walking about the ruins, Ingrid suddenly demanded that I write down "Titan—Jupiter or Zeus; Pan—Mars; Mesme—Venus." From my own knowledge of classical and prehistoric archaeology, I recognized the relationship between the Titans and Zeus, the Titans having been the precursors of the Olympian gods. Or, if the term were used as *the* Titan, then Zeus could be considered the son of Titan. The Pan-Mars relationship is not so well known, but it is true that Pan is considered a special aspect of the god Mars. Mesme as an alternate for Venus was totally new to me. Ingrid then drew three symbols representing the three gods she had mentioned: astrological symbols for Jupiter, Mars, and Venus. [Insert figure 5a.] These were drawn in a quaint, unusual style, quite unlike modern symbolism and certainly not something with which Ingrid would normally be familiar. In addition, she drew other symbols of which I will speak later.

"Fertility is a very important element here," Ingrid commented. "It also ties in with the young boys being sent through that ritualistic opening, because this is to represent fertility and the well-being of the people. The other god represents the elements—the sun and the wind and the things they feared, like floods and hurricanes. In other words, nature.

"I see three major subdivisions. The first would be religious—the religious nature of man. The second, the domestic nature of man—his well-being, including fertility. And the third would be the fearful part of nature. The latter would also have a great deal to do with crops and how they would grow, according to how one had treated the god for that year. If there had been too much rain, there wouldn't be any wheat. I think we should find some caves here indicating other rituals.

"I see long white robes worn by these people, tied at the waist and rather crudely made, and the people are barefoot. There are both men and women, with darkish hair, a little on the curly side, and darkish skin. They look Mediterranean or from Greece—something of that nature.

"As far as the caves are concerned, this one was the most spiritual one, because it deals with the mysteries—especially the mystery of death. I feel that here they wrote some of their ideas on the walls, asking for answers as to what happens after death, which was the most mysterious to them. Therefore, this is the most sacred area of the entire temple. I think the people who built this did not survive. It was a colony. They had a famine and disease, and died out."

I asked the important question that previously I had asked of others: "Where do they come from?"

"I think they were from either Greece or Mesopotamia," Ingrid answered.

We then arrived in front of the Sacrificial Table. I asked Ingrid to touch it and tell me what she felt. After a moment's hesitation, during which she let her hand glide along the groove in the table, she said, "I think if anything were sacrificed here it was no more than a lamb, and the reason was that they wanted to show that they had great abundance of everything, so they could waste it in that way. They were happy that they had been treated so well. I think that this table was used for gifts to the gods rather than sacrifices—symbolic gifts, in the form of food being prepared and put here for the gods to partake of."

"As you touch the table, do you get any impressions concerning the kind of people they were and the kind of language they spoke?" I asked.

"I get a different alphabet than ours. It almost looks like astrological symbols. I see a straight thing with prongs going out across the top," she told me.

I then asked Ingrid where she saw these symbols being written. "I see them on the wall," she responded. "I have the impression it is underground; it may even be hidden. The symbols represent the highest elements in their thoughts. I also see people with headbands around their heads. The material looks like papyrus . . . not really material, but a pounded wood of sorts. I think these rituals used a great amount of fire

Figure 5b. *Ingrid Beckman's symbols.*

and light. A lot of them were done in the evening and most of them in the dark—some at dawn—and I have the feeling they used big torches. Healing is also part of the rituals, and they heal by laying on hands. I get 1200 B.C. and have the impression of an Isis cult."

In addition to drawing the three symbols representing gods whom she had called Titan, Pan, and Mesme or Mesma, Ingrid then drew four more lines of symbols. There were two symbols in the first line, two in the second, three in the third line, and four in the fourth. Some of them were definitely astrological symbols. I was able to identify the symbols for the zodiacal signs of Pisces, Gemini, Aquarius, and Aries; the last line contained the symbol for the planet Neptune. However, the symbols didn't altogether make sense. It seemed that I had some sort of text before me, not merely a few astrological symbols, for several of them were definitely something else.

I felt highly elated that Ingrid had gotten such an early date, and I asked her to intensify her psychic search—to try and tell me where these people came from. "I'm getting an island, and I'm getting the Aegean," Ingrid replied.

When I asked her for the name of the island, she said, "Mesopotamia." This, of course, puzzled me, but she explained that the people from the island and from Mesopotamia were of one kind, in a manner of speaking, and that they were searching for the gods. "They felt that if they left their island they would find the home of the gods, and then they found this land."

"How did they come here?"

"In three ships. It was a small colony—not more than eighty people. They came to this spot—they chose it because it was the highest area."

"Can you get something on the leader's name?"

"I'm getting the word *Sina* or *Sinai*. These words are so different from our normal vocabulary because they end in vowels, like ai. A lot of these words are very short, with a lot of vowels in them." Ingrid walked a few steps further. "Everything these people did centered around a circle. They saw everything in terms of a circle. I see them chanting, and I see a person in the middle. They are wearing white robes. The one in the middle is a woman. She doesn't have a full robe on; she has a bare chest."

Immediately a thought flashed through my mind: there was only one place where priestesses worshiped bare-breasted rather than robed or fully nude—Minoan Crete! The ceremonial dress of high-status Cretan women, priestesses, and goddesses consisted only of a long, pleated skirt.

I directed Ingrid, who was getting more and more into the vibration of the place, to describe the ceremony she was seeing.

"I get the feeling [the woman] is supplicating the gods. She is using the power of the people around her. Each person carries a torch, and they are moving clockwise. There are other people sitting on the outskirts of this large circle, and they are all chanting according to her directions. I have the feeling she is asking for health and well-being for her people. Her arms are raised, and as the people are going around her clockwise, she is also going around clockwise in a smaller circle. There are fires on each side of it. She is the priestess. I see this happening in the main altar area, on a big slab of rock over there.

"A priest—the high priest—is standing by the official altar, while she is in the smaller circle. Then, all of a sudden, they all fall down. On the altar, I see one single taper. It's not a real candle—it's like a piece of weed. In a little phial, there is some sort of oil, and then I see some other things, like stalks of wheat. The priestess is above where we are now on this plateau. That is where the dance takes place. This is a ceremony for health, and after that they will do a more general ritual for the whole community. This refers to the crops. The priest's part is almost like a speech. It isn't the same physical thing she is doing. She is really raising energy, while he is not. He is more ceremonial, more talking than acting, but they work together as a team.

"After this, there is time for pleasantries among the people. Food is cooked on open fires; the people mingle with each other. This will go on all night until dawn, when it is over. This happens once or twice a year—not very often, because it is a high ceremony. It is a seasonal festival. The children who were going through that opening were ahead of these other ceremonies; they were the beginning of it. It is almost like a May Day celebration."

What Ingrid had described so vividly was nothing less than an authentic pagan ritual. In this ceremony, a priestess would turn in a circle and the community would do likewise around her. Using this "wheel," the ancients would raise psychic energy to direct it where it was needed. I doubted very much that Ingrid knew this, however, astute as she might have been concerning present-day occult practices.

"Was there any human sacrifice practiced in this area of the complex?" I asked. "Were any fertility rituals performed here?"

Ingrid shook her head. "I don't see any human sacrifices. I see little boys going through the area and coming out and showing themselves to the crowd along with a particular music—and certain events leading up to this."

We sat down on one of the larger stones, and Ingrid closed her eyes for a moment. She continued, "They were so pagan that they felt if they left their island they could find the home of the gods, and that is why they started out in these boats. They were not wooden boats, but boats with things tied together like bushels—banana-shaped, with square sails and some oars. Finally, they came upon this land, and they were disappointed because they searched and couldn't find the gods. They tried to draw the gods closer to them by building up this area here, but in the end they were defeated because they weren't able to get enough food. Then there was this cold climate, and they weren't used to it. I don't think they had ever seen snow before."

We continued our inspection and walked up to the roof of the largest "cave." I asked Ingrid what she felt had happened in this area.

"I think this was an area for some of the people to watch from," she replied. "Down there, the special people, the ones who were participating, did their work. It felt like a large arena. But, I meant to tell you . . . while I was sitting on those stones, I kept getting a word; it was *Cufu*, and it seems to represent some abstract thing—either a shrine to a deity or a deity itself."

The great pyramid of Cufu, or Khufu, is one of Egypt's continuing puzzles. We don't even know when it was built or by whom. The assumption that an early Egyptian pharaoh named Khufu, or Chefren, constructed it is not necessarily correct. He may have found it and used it, or those who came after him may have used it as a burial monument for the pharaoh. Khufu was, in the Egyptian manner, also considered a god or a god-king. Of course, he lived a great deal earlier than the 1200 B.C. date mentioned by Ingrid.

I wondered if Ingrid didn't mean the word *Keftiu*. This was a term used by the Egyptians for the people of Minoan Crete, according to H.E.L. Mellerish in *Minoan Crete*. Also, when she mentioned the word *Sina* or *Sinai* in the investigation, perhaps she was referring to Sitia, a major town in eastern Crete.

I asked Ingrid if her impressions were similar to ghostly presences, or if they were strictly psychometric impressions from the past, without any life in the present. "I think they are more psychometric impressions from the past," she answered. "And those letters that I drew were very crudely done. I think [the originals] were done in stone and were kind of rusty yellow or gray in color."

I then asked Ingrid where the strange characters she had drawn for me earlier had been engraved. "I see a stone with these characters incised in it, perhaps a quarter of an inch thick," she replied.

"There are at least eight characters on this stone. As I was going around these caves, I saw certain caves marked for different gods, like Pan, Mesma, and Titan. However, besides those caves for the three gods, there are different caves for other rituals. I kept feeling four corners for the other four gods, who are more abstract than the [first] three gods. In order to appease the three major gods and the four 'corners,' the people had four separate caves at four different spots for the gods to live in. There are no actual rituals involved in those caves, but no one is allowed to go into them because they are sacred to the gods.

"I also had the distinct impression, while I was walking around, that this site has many levels, religious as well as astrological. I feel that they took sightings and bearings on the stars from here and also from the sun. They took sightings of an astronomical nature. I think they lined up the rocks. They lined up the rocks with the rising of the sun and the setting of the sun and also with several major stars."

I was flabbergasted by this. Since we had not yet left the central area of the site, Ingrid knew nothing about the monoliths in the outer perimeter that had to do with astronomical alignments. Nor had she read anything about the excavations at Mystery Hill. There was no way she could have known about the astronomical purpose of the complex or about the stones used for alignments.

I took Ingrid down the steps to the Megaron House, considered the largest structure of the complex (see photo 27). She touched the walls and turned to me with increased excitement in her voice. "It is like Stonehenge," she said. "I'm getting distinctly the word *Sendar*. I've been getting this three or four times now. I'm also getting the word *Mesme*, and it feels like a female deity. Then there is another word—it is a god again, and it starts with *A*. It is a male god, sounding like Aron. This Aron is connected with Mesme.

"I have the impression that this chamber has something to do with young maidens. I see young girls around here, and it is a frivolous thing. It has something to do with the coming of spring. It is also tied in with fertility worship. I believe the girls went into this chamber. It was almost like a christening, to show that they were of age. One or two at a time would go in there. They would just go in and be blessed by the gods and then come out again. There would be no one else in there. They would just walk in and out as a ceremonial ritual to show that they had come of age. Then they would join the rest of the people in a big festival, something like a May Day festival. That is the fertility festival in the spring, and the community joins in it.

"There are several maidens each year that go through this. There is dancing and festivities and drinking, and all this comes to a climax when these girls are being initiated in here. I see older women putting flowers in their hair now, and they are coming from this direction, going in here, and then turning around and going out again. After that, they walk up to the main altar to be seen by the whole group. They are dressed modestly in white robes, with flowers in their hair, and they are presented to the group. This comes after the children have run through this opening, as I mentioned earlier, because that shows fertility. I mean, it shows birth and then the entry into adulthood.

"After that, I see the high priestess doing the healing for the entire community—a symbolic healing. This is followed by the priest at the altar; there is wine and barley on the altar. He is speaking and is very intense. After that, there is a lot of noise, like clapping and chanting, and the whole community joins in. Then they disperse into small groups and go off.

"There was a building—the walls were much higher than they are now—and it had a roof over it made of timbers. I have the feeling it was reserved for the elders of the community, because they were more respected. They sat here and talked about future movements and the crops and so on."

Ingrid and I walked over to the surrounding wall at the extreme end of the complex. There was a moment of peace, and I asked Ingrid to try and give me details about the people who had come here from afar.

"They came from an island," she repeated, "a large island."

"Was theirs the only town on the island?" I asked.

"No, there are other towns. I get Crete. I have no conscious visualization of where these things are."

"What are these people called? What is their civilization called?" I probed.

"I'm going to say Minoan. I'll say Minos, but that's more like a king. Minoan, and I want to say empire now."

While I was pondering this momentous statement, Ingrid and I walked further away from the main site toward the outer perimeter. At one point, Ingrid touched one of the stones, which seemed to have some sort of crude markings on it. "Look," she said, "these incisions—I think this one resembles or is supposed to indicate a woman. For some reason, the two circles represent a woman to me." As I was thinking of the possibility that it represented a primitive mother goddess, we were interrupted by Robert Stone, who had walked up the hill to join us.

Stone explained that they had indeed found a number of inscribed stones, but that the association had placed them in the museum of the administration building for reasons of safety. "Unless the stones are monstrously large, we carry them out," he said. "We have one showing something like a ship, and I also want to show you an engraved stone in the large cave."

I asked Stone to bring me up to date on the latest developments at Mystery Hill. "We've cleaned the swamp from the ramp, and we've discovered that when we set up the north stone it lines up with another stone, the summer solstice stone for June 22," he told me. "It's right on the button, too. We have discovered that true north is exactly across the Sacrificial Table, where we had expected it to be. However, the reference point, the point for viewing these stones, is just slightly north of the table, where the old cross is. They line up also. We haven't yet cleared all the paths for the sunrise stone, and only one stone is still missing."

"How large would you say the entire area of the ancient observatory was?" I queried.

"From the stones we are finding, I would estimate it to be around fifteen acres," he answered.

Fortunately Robert Stone and the association own all that land. In fact, they have bought another parcel of land to the northwest since my last visit. The reason for this additional purchase was that they discovered interesting artifacts on the ground and felt that they should safeguard the acreage. Thus, they have added another twelve to fifteen acres to the Mystery Hill complex.

"What puzzles us," Stone continued, "is the question of where the people lived who built this place. In what direction from the site and how far from it did they live?"

I turned to Ingrid for any psychic impressions she might have. "They didn't live right on the site," she explained. "This entire site was so sacred that they did not live here, but they did come from within eight miles of this place. There may be other remnants of this settlement in the area that are yet to be discovered, but this complex is the main thing, the religious end of it."

Stone then took us to the sunrise stone, which was a little bit afield from the main complex. Archaeologists had not found anything in the way of artifacts in that direction. I asked Ingrid to touch the stone to see whether she would get any impressions from it. "I see someone writing something down—a man—and it seems as if he is checking some calculations." Stone wondered whether Ingrid wasn't getting an impression of himself, four weeks back, when he was standing at the exact spot, writing something down!

"This area is where we believe the Sacrificial Table came from," Stone explained. "The construction and the kind of stone pretty much fit. Also, the table is the right size for having come from this area. We think 'they' removed the first layer of bedrock from here to build the site. That is how we dated it through our radiocarbon tests. The charcoal came from above the worked bedrock. Prior to the time when the charcoal flowed in, somebody had already worked the bedrock. It checks out at 2000 B.C., so we know for sure that people lived here at that time. The other reading checked out to 1200 B.C."

"Twelve hundred B.C.," Ingrid said. "That is exactly what I got when I first saw the site." I wondered whether she was referring to the period when Mystery Hill was at its cultural height or to when its culture was beginning to fade.

NEARA was trying to survey the walls surrounding the principal site, which was quite a formidable task. They were quite sure that the walls were man-made and that they were already in existence when Pattee bought the place in the nineteenth century. Unfortunately, an aerial survey would not help, because trees currently reached nearly to the top of the hill.

"There are more structures to the northwest that need to be looked at," Stone told us. "Near the town of Kingston, not too far away from here, there is an underground structure in existence that is similar to the one here. However, it is completely collapsed now. This wasn't just a small culture centering around Mystery Hill. We have located over two hundred underground chambers, all made of the same type of stone, in New England. However, there is only one other site that compares at all with Mystery Hill in size, and that is at Groton, Connecticut. There is no temple, but there is a double circle of stones that we think may have been used to grind corn or to drive an animal around with a wheel." Ingrid reminded me that she had also felt someone grinding corn in one of the places at Mystery Hill, and Stone confirmed that this was NEARA's assumption, too.

As we walked around the outer perimeter, Stone pointed at the various menhirs—those silent, yet eloquent hewn stones set up specifically to serve as markers for the observatory. "I got in touch with Gerald Hawkins, the expert on Stonehenge, and told him of our counterpart. He wrote back saying that if the alignment of our stones was more than plus or minus five degrees above or below the horizon to forget it. So we had to measure them and survey the entire area. We found that, from this vantage point, every one of them was right on the button, on the far distant horizon. Looking downhill, the horizon is way off and too high, but we measured in the winter when there was no greenery on the trees. Even these measurements were within three to four degrees of the horizon. We did find three out of four stones; the fourth one may have been lost or hasn't been discovered yet. I'm talking about the large menhirs, the ones that would mark the solstices. Perhaps the fourth was destroyed or carted away." I looked to where Stone pointed, and saw clearly the large summer solstice stone standing in the middle of the swath.

We then turned out attention to the Oracle Chamber. I wanted to check on some of the things Ingrid had said about it prior to Stone's arrival. I asked her if there was any evidence, archaeologically speaking, that ashes had been placed in it. "They used this as a religious chamber," she answered, "and they could have put either a body or ashes in the cubbyhole, or closet, here." I mentioned to Stone that Ingrid had not seen any human sacrifices connected with the Sacrificial Table—only animal sacrifices. That was Stone's view also.

Stone then pointed to the left, where the excavation administration had placed the letter *J* as a marker, to the carving of what appeared to be a ship (see photo 28). I asked Ingrid for her impressions of it. "It looks like the ship I described to you before—the ship I saw them coming over in," she said excitedly. "It was a long ship that looked like a banana, and it was made of things tied together, like bundles. It had a square sail and was very primitive." There was no doubt about it. Ingrid had described the ship before she had seen the carving.

"Ingrid thought that no one was ever buried here," I said to Stone. "Have you ever found any bones?"

"We once found a fragment and checked it out with the Smithsonian a few years ago, but there have been no skeletons and no graves," he responded. "However, there is a tradition that skulls should be found near the cliff that is part of this site. The story goes that people used to find skulls there, but all we found were some broken Indian arrows and pieces of a clay vessel. It was all American Indian, yet we never found an Indian artifact at the site of the ruins themselves. Indians roamed the entire area, but they must have had a reason for staying away from the hill."

I thought it ludicrous that some establishment archaeologists would shrug off the ruins at Mystery Hill as being American Indian in origin when the American Indians themselves would have no part of it. Besides, American Indians in New England never used stones to build houses in this manner.

It was getting dark, so we decided to return to the administration building. There, Stone pointed out several inscribed stones taken from the walls on the hill. I asked Ingrid to touch one of them to see what she would derive from it, psychometrically speaking. "I think it has something to do with burial or death," she said. "Something to do with the philosophy of death, but it is not a burial stone."

I asked Ingrid to touch the next stone. She said, "I think this is a marker, and it has something to do with astronomy."

Next, I asked Ingrid to touch a triangular stone that had some kind of writing on it, a stone that had attracted me the very first time I had set foot on the site. Ingrid, of course, couldn't possibly read the inscription. "This has something to do with prophecy and oracles," she announced. "It says something about oracles coming from the gods, being the gift from the gods, from the Triad. [They are] a way for the gods to speak directly to the people, to tell them how they are doing and what they should change."

I next asked Ingrid to touch a small stone that seemed to have one letter inscribed on it. "I feel this is symbolic of the hunt," she said. The letter resembled a Roman C.

We went on to the next stone, which seemed to have some sort of incision in it, but Ingrid received no impression from it. "Remember," she said, "I also saw arrows and something tied to a handle, like a large rock tied to a handle. This rock looks like that."

Stone took us to an opposite wall, where he showed us a whole row of primitive tools—stone picks and other implements—that were found in one chamber, all piled up in one corner. He thought the fact that they were found all together rather than haphazardly scattered around the site was very important. He called another inscribed stone a "rubbing stone" and believed it to be an implement connected with the grinding of corn. When he mentioned this, Ingrid nodded immediately. She "saw" that precise activity taking place.

My attention was drawn to a series of crystals. These were crystals found in what the association calls a "well" but which might have been an ancient mine shaft. Stone mentioned that the analysis of one of the crystals turned up something rather strange. "The gray powdery layer and the thin, dark-brownish layer are two different substances: one is aluminum and the other is silver. The chemists don't know why they are attached to the crystals, and I'm having them sent to a friend of mine at Massachusetts Institute of Technology for further analysis." (These were rough stones, the sides of which had crystallized due to aging and other natural processes.) Further analysis confirmed earlier findings on the age of the stones.

Next, we were shown some very ancient pottery that Stone felt was used at the site. It was probably produced from the clay in the swamp. Somewhat excitedly, Ingrid pointed at it. "The thing I saw in the chamber, that red pot, was shaped just like that," she said. She meant the pot in which the ashes had been placed.

Stone seemed interested in Ingrid's disclosure. "Frank Glynn, when he was president of the Connecticut Archaeological Society, also envisioned pots because of the pottery pieces that were found. He thought pretty much along the same lines."

Through Robert Stone, we met Sally Johansen, who has helped with the digs at Mystery Hill ever since she "discovered" it in 1967. In addition to being an amateur archaeologist, Johansen is psychic. "I always had the feeling that I was coming home to the hill," she explained. "Also, that it is much older than the carbon dating indicates. My feeling is that it is about thirty-five thousand years old, not just four thousand years old."

"What makes you think so?" I asked.

"I've had the feeling that there were little bands of people around here," she said. "I found a stone with an open eye on it and another with a winking eye on it. And there is a ledge in one section of Mystery Hill where there is a stone with two eyes, one open and one winking. Even the Phoenicians left from here to go to other parts of the world. [They] didn't come from the Middle East and arrive here; they left here and went to other parts of the world where they developed a culture and became more sophisticated."

I wasn't sure whether I had heard her correctly. "Are you saying that these Semitic cultures originated in the Americas?"

"Yes. At one time there was an ocean where the Rockies are now, and ships could sail through it. What are now the mountains of New Hampshire were then small islands surrounded by water, and people went back and forth from Mystery Hill to other hills and ships. I think this was an island, and the culture was on top."

Johansen explained that she had been to Mexico three times to study ancient cultures. She had found certain parallels between Cuautla, in central Mexico, and what she knew about Mystery Hill. For that reason, she felt that bands of people left Mystery Hill and went south, possibly to Mexico. I then showed her the strange characters drawn by Ingrid while she was examining the rocks at Mystery Hill and asked her if she had ever seen anything like them before. Immediately she nodded. "Yes. The two lines that look like the zodiac symbol for Aquarius have to do with lightning. This is similar to Cuautlan symbols I have seen."

After this visit to Mystery Hill, the little crystal given me by Robert Stone continued to fascinate me. I decided to subject it to a number of psychometric tests with mediumistic individuals—without, of course, telling them what they were reading or where it had come from.

I handed the crystal to Shawn Robbins and asked him about the origins of the people who had used it. He replied, "I see a man in some sort of Latin costume; it could be Mexican."

To test Ingrid Beckman's ability to pick out an item regardless of its surroundings, I asked her to psychometrize three different objects enclosed in envelopes and marked only with initials. There was no way she could visually deduce anything about the envelopes' contents. "I am getting some impressions of the United States from this item," she said immediately about the envelope containing the crystal, "and I think it is from New Hampshire. I'm getting something about Minos and Greece and religion and a religious site and astrology." These comments were amazing, considering that this test occurred several months after Ingrid's visit to Mystery Hill. Nothing in my conversation with her would have indicated my intention to test her on an object from that site.

On June 11, 1975, exactly one year after Ingrid's visit to the site, I asked her once more to psychometrize some objects for me. The crystal, camouflaged by tissue paper, evoked the following comments: "I get California . . . a group of pagans. Ceremonies are done in this spot, mainly by young people. This stone is supposed to be used as a tool. I see a woman in her late forties in a long robe that is brown, and I hear the word *Eko*. It is an outdoor site where rituals went on for many years. It goes back to 1200 B.C. I think of Diana and lunar astrology, of herbology and the West Coast. This is an arid area, and high. The present group is mixed but white. The woman may be English or Scottish. I get the name Aronk or Aron. There are eleven people . . . a young man with short hair, thin, who is interested in astrology. Most of the others are in their late twenties or thirties. I think of Santa Barbara. The woman has founded this group. You [meaning Hans] met her three years ago and have been to the Covensted twice. The words *Druid* and *Eros*. There was more than one culture in the area; they were overlapping. I think of Ethiopia and agrarian culture. Everything was laid out for a particular purpose: the passing of time, the calendar, the fear of the seasons. There were fertility rites, and the mother is very important."

This curious reading was a mixed bag. On analyzing it, I found that Ingrid had read simultaneously two different layers of consciousness. On the one hand, she spoke quite clearly of the sanctuary at Mystery Hill. Her information was exact, even to mentioning the same date and the

name of one of the deities or individuals connected with the site—Aronk
or Aron (Ares)—that she had mentioned during her visit to the site. On
the other hand, she described a contemporary meeting of a pagan group
in California and placed me with it. This, too, was entirely correct, for
I had been to California prior to the test.

Lastly, I tested the crystal with Nancy Abel, a young but highly tal-
ented psychic. She had had ESP flashes for many years and had an intense interest in developing them. Upon handing her the crystal, I asked
her to give me her immediate impressions. Nancy knew nothing about
the origin of the crystal, nor my reasons for being interested in it. Feeling she would do better alone, she took the crystal into the next room
and wrote down her impressions. Her notes stated as follows:

1. cave
2. from a different planet, not earthlings
3. Inca
4. war
5. civilization from the past

This psychic might have said almost anything concerning the piece
of stone, which certainly did not offer any visual clues about its origin
or purpose. The fact that she came up with five images that were later
borne out by Ethel Johnson Meyers's visit to Mystery Hill was extraordinary.

ETHEL MEYERS VISITS MYSTERY HILL

To continue my in-depth research into the origins of Mystery Hill, I traveled to the site with Ethel Johnson Meyers on November 12, 1974. In addition to being a clairvoyant and psychometrist like Ingrid Beckman, Ethel was probably one of the best deep-trance mediums to ever work in the United States. She had a fine reputation with various scientists and allowed herself to become an instrument through which discarnates might speak. Whenever I took Ethel to a promising site, things always happened. I never had a failure in the sense that nothing came through her. If the site had vibrations from the past, or if a trapped entity clung to it, Ethel made contact with these energies. In addition to her trance work, she was a very good clairvoyant, and thus I looked forward to a "double exposure" of the ruins at Mystery Hill through Ethel's psychic abilities.

Our flight from New York was uneventful, but the rainy weather left a great deal to be desired. This did not deter Ethel, who was a very good trooper—perhaps a throwback to her days as a vaudeville star, when she traveled in all weathers and conditions. We were properly dressed for the rainy day and decided not to let the rain stop us from doing what we came to do. As I had done with Ingrid, I made sure that Ethel knew nothing about the project. Even when Dorothy Stone picked us up at the airport, the conversation was carefully steered away from anything to do with Mystery Hill. Thus, Ethel's first contact with the ruins came when she stood in front of them. However, she began getting impressions about them even as we were trudging up the last few yards of the hill. As soon as we had established "headquarters" in the midst of the Mystery Hill complex, I asked Ethel to let her psychic fonts flow.

"A few redheads, a few redheads," she mumbled the minute I turned my tape recorder on. "But I also saw [sic] some light-skinned people—

three of them—down there by this table under which I think fires were built."

"Did you hear anything?"

"When I was coming up the path, I thought I heard something like *yami, yami*. And then another word that sounded like *oogala*."

"What language is it?"

"I don't think it's Indian."

Just then I remembered how she had turned to me on the plane to Boston and said something about a foreign language. That was when we were still two hours away from the site. "Yes," Ethel confirmed, "it was on the plane that I heard this strange language. It sounded like *reeshee-hoo-ee, reeshee-hoo-ee* or *hoo-ye*."

Ethel looked around the site with a quizzical expression. "Have there been any underground tunnels discovered here?" she asked. I confirmed that there had been. "Well, there are quite a few more than what they've found."

Then she "saw" some more people with her inner eye and began to describe them. "There are these taller people, and then there are also a lot of very small people. They are darker. The tall people are white, and some of them have reddish hair. I saw three redheads. There are two different sorts of people here. But it looks as if the white people are the bosses."

"Did they live here at the same time or at different times?"

"I think perhaps the small people were overtaken by something else. The white people are the strangers."

"Where are they from?"

"Nordic. They keep saying, '*Yama, yama, yama.*' '*Yama mekoty.*' And then something that sounds like *pzht*."

"How far back do they go?"

"1800 B.C." Ethel was touching one of the stones now and mumbling something I didn't quite catch. I asked her to repeat it. "*Rit-me-i-a-tooi*. And another word, *ishma*. There are two kinds of people here. I see them as solidly as anything. I think they visited here."

"Where from?"

"This is somehow related to Stonehenge. These are outer space individuals; they come and go. Polaris, Albert says."

Albert was Ethel's spirit guide. Whenever she was in doubt about her impressions, she asked him, and frequently he had the answers. Whenever she would go into full trance, Albert watched over her so that no unwanted entity would use the medium's faculties.

"Why did they come here?"

"To help the indigenous population, which is dark and small."

"Why did they come to this spot?"

"Someone was lost here, and the others came to the rescue."

"How did they get here? By what means of transportation?"

"Dematerialization."

"Did they come from some other place on Earth?"

"They stopped off at different places. There was a terrible deluge. The indigenous people came up here to escape. Everything was washed out, like in the middle of an ocean. The Earth's axis was to the west. Radioactive sunrays caused floods—polar floods."

At this point, a slight drizzle began, but it didn't stop us.

"What did they try to build here?"

"Sun worship. Iron crosses. To worship the sun . . . the indigenous individuals."

"What did the foreigners worship?"

"Nothing outside of themselves. The northwest end of Atlantis was their first stomping ground—broken off from Greenland under the water. That was their home. Some branches went out to Egypt, to the southern tip of this continent, and to South America."

"How did they leave here, and what became of them?"

"Dematerialized. Those who were marooned by the great flood went forth to take care of themselves. When they learn how to respect the inner intelligence and know that all things that come from the sun are the enlightened way to find the inner self . . . the inner being is the godly part of you. . . . They are bothering him, they will hardly let him speak, the little ones. They want to be noticed."

I realized that Albert had practically taken over Ethel and that she was no longer speaking as herself. I decided to leave philosophy alone and try to get some hard facts. "Where do these white-skinned people come from?"

"From Polaris, the north star. They live not on the star, but in the universe around it. A planet. Yahitma is their planet. Yahitma Hooh! I don't know what it means."

"What is the language they are speaking?"

"Here we term it Atlantean. There it is Yahitma Hooh."

"Is this place just a temple, or was it used for other purposes?"

"It was a temple to learn and to find the mysteries inside oneself. One sits in positions to learn how to leave the body."

"Why were these tunnels built?"

"These are secret chambers where rituals were undertaken into the highest initiations, that they might go forth and teach in their turn: learning to travel between outer space and here, leaving the physical body asleep, and finally, to dematerialize it altogether and remove it to other places. Teachings went as far north as Alaska, which was then warmer."

The rain had gotten to be quite heavy by this time, and I suggested we walk back to the administration building. As we returned slowly over the slippery ground, Ethel explained that natives of the Earth later came to destroy the sanctuary. They were what we would call Indians, and they were very much afraid of it. Then Ethel saw the little men forming a symbol that reminded her of a cross further up on the site, and she asked to go there.

"They are doing some sort of dance," she reported. "It looks almost Egyptian. Now they are putting their hands up."

"What sort of clothes are these people wearing?"

"Not much—like hanging from the shoulder."

"What about the white-skinned people? How are they dressed?"

"Very much different—light colored from shoulder to knee." Ethel stood transfixed, staring at something only she could see. "They are doing a dance up there. It is a ritual of some kind, as if they are grasping for the sun."

Suddenly she turned to me with a very puzzled expression, as if I had the answer to what she saw with her inner eye. "Why are there boats here—those funny, long, wooden boats?" she asked.

I asked her to describe the boats in detail.

"They kind of go up, have a high part in the front. I don't see any sails. They look like Viking boats."

Ethel then went on to describe the crude lines on one of the stones as the face of a priest with a high hat. I followed her eyes and, sure enough, I saw it too. "He looks very Egyptian," Ethel remarked, "and, come to think of it, those dark people look more Egyptian than Indian."

Despite the rain, we walked further through the swath in the trees until we stood at the north solstice stone. Ethel touched it and went into a semitrance, ignoring the rain completely. After a minute or two, which seemed like an eternity in the downpour, she opened her eyes and relaxed. I asked her what she had felt when she touched the stone.

"This is sacred ground," she replied solemnly. "This is burial ground all the way down here." Earlier, Ethel had asked whether any bones had been found here. Robert Stone had explained that after all this time, and in this kind of soil, bones would have oxidized after about fifty years, so the likelihood of finding any was nil.

Ethel pointed to the solstice stone and the faint carving on it, which she said looked like a seal or sea lion. I wondered why people in these hills would have carvings of sea animals. She answered, "They were surrounded by water. There was a flood."

We left the stone and went back toward the center of the site. At the Sacrificial Table, I asked Ethel to put her hands on the rim and listen with her psychic ears.

"It is like screaming," she said. "*Ye-zha-hish-da. Ya koe.*"

"What is happening on this table?"

"There was a sundial here somewhere, and there has been sacrifice, but it is terribly hated. The dark people, the small ones, are doing it. There is fighting, and then the white-skinned people are coming down like thunder out of the sky."

"What about the subterranean chamber in the back of the table? What is this for, in your opinion?"

"Torture, but it has been turned into something more fruitful." Again, Ethel laid her hands on the Sacrificial Table, but withdrew them quickly. "Oh, I've got to close my ears. This groove is an Egyptian symbol put here so that it may not happen again. . . . Actions against the wild man, the indigenous man, who doesn't know what he commits on others is retroactive to him."

"What are these people called?"

"Miki-aku."

"What happened here?"

"The heart was taken out first in the sacrifice. They liked most often little children, about three to five years old. It is for the great sun god up there."

"What is the name of the sun god?"

"Mu."

"What do they call their homeland, these people who came here from abroad?"

"Egypt. There was a great leader. Heyt . . . Hayd . . . I can't quite get it. This is after Atlantis was gone. What remained was England, Ireland, Spain, part of Italy, the Azores, Bimini."

I asked Ethel to touch one of the other stones. "Outer space individuals," she mumbled. "This is another language . . . *Ye-yhist-a-him-i. Ye-yhist-a-him-i Ya-ki-wha.* That is what it sounds like. There are two names: Ya-him-i, He-ma."

"What does Albert feel these engraved stones were for?"

"What they taught: to live within themselves and to respect the inner high self. The initiates came to help, and they have done a very magnificent, self-sacrificing job on these heathens."

The rain was getting too heavy now, so we decided to seek the shelter of the administration building after all. As we hurried down the slope, Ethel told me that she felt that the rows of stones were markers to be seen from the sky, similar to those found in South America.

After some hot tea and a quiet session between Ethel Meyers and Betty Hill (the heroine of John Fuller's *Interrupted Journey*), who had come down from Portsmouth for a sitting, we returned to New York.

I have already mentioned that Ethel Johnson Meyers had a spirit control or guide: her first husband, Albert. Many times Albert was able to give information that the medium herself was unable to supply. However, at times, I tried to pry information loose from Albert that I was unable to obtain from another discarnate entity speaking through Ethel, only to be frustrated by Albert's insistence that he could not divulge what the principal in the matter would not want to. On the whole, though, Albert had a dispassionate view of the scene and frequently supplied an orderly picture of what was going on, thus supplementing Ethel's own observations both in and out of trance in a most valuable way.

On December 3, 1974, I met with Ethel in her studio in New York City for the purpose of inducing communication with Albert concerning Mystery Hill. I had brought the crystal along to serve as an inducer and to make the contact stronger, if that was necessary. As he had done many times over the years, Albert took over Ethel's speech mechanism in a matter of two or three minutes, manifesting a clearly distinct personality from Ethel's own. After the amenities of greeting had been attended to, I asked Albert to tell me whatever he might know beyond the information that Ethel herself had revealed concerning the nature, background, names, origin, and period of the people who had lived at Mystery Hill.

Albert explained that there were several layers of people related to Mystery Hill, one on top of the other, and that he would give me his explanation of them chronologically.

"First of all, there have been what you might call the aborigines, related to the early people who have come out of Egypt. They have been transported to the far west by the Atlanteans before the great flood. They brought them there to populate the world and distribute humanity better and to give them dependence upon themselves. These people came from places like Egypt, Libya, Iran, the Mesopotamian valley, and were not very knowledgeable people. The Atlanteans were the master race at the time. They were people from outer space who had come and settled and felt it their duty to educate the early individuals. This happened about twenty thousand years B.C."

"How did they transfer these people to the various places?"

"They had a possibility that is still being searched for. They could dematerialize the physical body of an individual and rematerialize it. They could collapse space and time and send people to different parts of the globe."

"Did any of the people of Mystery Hill come from the Mediterranean?"

"The earliest people at the hill were from Mesopotamia, and they came as far north as New Hampshire as well as all the way down to the Yucatán. The second people were Egyptians, and they built this temple at the beginning of the Piscean Age. This was before the great deluge, and this high ground just happened to be above the water line. The purpose of the temple was, as in Egypt, to teach and initiate others into the knowledge of how to use their own natural laws. They were small people, dark but not black. Eventually, they were mischief makers, because the deluge came and left them stranded, and so they quarreled. They destroyed each other, and the Atlanteans themselves came to make peace amongst them. The Atlanteans did not live here; they merely came to oversee and to take care. They were people with light complexion and titian-colored hair—some of it reddish—and they were rather tall."

"What happened next here, chronologically?"

"When things had settled down, the more elite Egyptians came and there was a long period of prosperity. This was around 18,000 B.C., and by that time the waters had receded a good deal. However, sea life was left near here, and it was held in great reverence. They did not find it difficult to travel back and forth.

"Then there is another layer, and this one is Nordic. This would be between 15,000 and 12,000 B.C. Atlantis was to the north in the Atlantic Ocean near Iceland and Greenland, part of the Scandinavian countries. The Nordic people arrived in boats."

"Who came after that?"

"People from the Mediterranean, who also arrived in boats. By that time, the powers of Atlantis had lost their effect upon those who would travel in the manner of the Atlanteans and early Egyptians."

"Where did the Mediterranean people start out from?"

"They came from Phoenicia and the southern tip of Macedonia, from the Aegean Islands and part of what today is Turkey. This happened between 12,000 and 10,000 B.C. They remained a very long time. Finally, the American Indians came. But the American Indians had nothing to do with this tribe."

"How did the world of the Mediterranean people come to an end? Did they just go away, or did they die out?"

"They became part of the indigenous population, but finally lost their traditions. This, of course, took thousands of years. It happened between 8000 and 4000 B.C."

"Are there any artifacts left that have not been discovered?"

"There are caved-in tunnels leading to other places, caches of treasure, things that have been stored away. This is to the northwest and the southwest. There is a tunnel between the two points starting with the center of the compound."

"Was there a connection between Mystery Hill and any other monument?"

"That is exactly what I am speaking of. But it is thoroughly buried, because the tunnels have caved in."

"What was the purpose of the so-called Sacrificial Table?"

ETHEL MEYERS

"It had various meanings through the years. The earliest arrivals built the Sacrificial Table, but many different people used it. The tribes fought amongst themselves and were eventually dominated by one called Peekawaukoo."

"Were those Indians?"

"No, they were the little ones. They were vicious toward each other, and they sacrificed to their great spirits. The Atlanteans came to stop this massacre, and when the little ones were brought into submission, under the Atlanteans, there was a dwindling away. They could no longer enjoy their sacrifices, their brutalities, so after the waters receded they began to move into different parts of the world. Again they are [*sic*] physically picked up, dematerialized, and placed into different places by the Atlanteans. Some of them are put down in the Yucatán, some of them in Arizona, and some in South America. But the temple had been built, and, when the people from Egypt arrived, they began to offer sacrifices of animals here."

"Prior to that, it was used for human sacrifice?"

"That is right."

I thanked Albert for the information and brought Ethel out of her trance. Ethel had now supplied not only an interesting narrative, some of which was certainly beyond any objective proof, but also phonetic chunks of a strange language that could be evaluated.

Shortly before Ethel Johnson Meyers passed on to the Higher Realms, when she was well into her nineties, she told me that in her mind there had always been a link between "extraterrestrial visitors" and the strange people she had seen psychically at Mystery Hill, who she had often referred to as people from Atlantis. She wanted me to know that to the Indians in New Hampshire's past, Mystery Hill was as much a mystery as it is to us now.

At this point, I would like to compare the theories of various scholars about Mystery Hill. In discussing the famous Bat Creek stone with its Aramaic inscription in *Strange Creatures from Time and Space*, John Keel pointed out that both Dr. Joseph B. Mahan and Dr. Cyrus Gordon believe the Hebrews might have reached the American continent during the Bronze Age.

Both scientists speculate that ancient Semitic tribes from the East may have visited North America thousands of years ago. This, of course, provides memories of the Lost Tribe of Israel. Could they have somehow found their way to this continent and become that lost American culture described in the Mormon Bible? Dr. Mahan believes that some Indian tribes can be traced back to seafaring Mediterranean peoples. The Yuchi, he points out, are racially and linguistically different from other North American tribes. Their legend states, "We came as the sun came, and we went as the sun went." Dr. Mahan interprets this to mean that the Yuchi came from the East, across the Atlantic Ocean, and then moved northward from Florida to Georgia.

Charles Michael Boland said in *They All Discovered America*:

The first discoverer of America . . . was of Asiatic ancestry. A Stone Age nomad, unskilled and uncivilized, unlettered . . . remained static until a diffusion of cultures from across the seas taught him the higher arts he was incapable of developing himself. He came across or around the huge glacier which engulfed a great part of North America, but left Alaska ice free.

According to Boland, this happened between 35,000 and 18,000 B.C. He continued:

The second discoverer of America arrived in a ship from the Mediterranean and left a record of his visit in a rubble of stones on a New Hampshire hillside. He resembled the first, or Stone Age discoverer, only in that his name has not been made known to us. He came leading a mournful band of religious freedom seekers during the first millennium before the birth of Christ. Others of his kind came at later times but for different reasons, and they, in turn, left records of their visits in scattered stones and ruins near the banks of the Susquehanna, in Pennsylvania, and on steaming jungle rocks deep in Brazil. The most overwhelming traces of these visits are strewn all over the New Hampshire landscape just outside North Salem, about fifty miles northwest of Boston.

Boland was speaking, of course, of Mystery Hill. He pointed out that the Neolithic people of Egypt, who were already adept at writing, taxation, and conquering, had begun to investigate the idea of marine travel on a large scale. About 3200 B.C., they recorded their first sea voyage. They sent a fleet of forty ships over to Phoenicia to get cedar wood, and they may have used it to build their first real seagoing vessels.

Eventually, another people took over the task of building ships and exploring the seas. These were the Cretans. They were dominant in the field until a great natural disaster destroyed much of Crete between 1400 and 1200 B.C.

> Control of the Mediterranean now fell jointly to the Greeks and Phoenicians. Of the two inheritors, the Phoenicians were by far the more aggressive and inquisitive, and from their home ports of Tyre and Sidon, they roamed the Mediterranean. . . . By 1200 B.C. they had reached the Straits of Gibraltar.

In the fourth century B.C., a Greek mariner named Pythes reached Britain in search of tin. He even managed to sail further, to an island called Ultima Thule, and wrote two books about it. What he had reached is modern Iceland. Of this there is no doubt, according to Boland.

The Phoenicians and Norsemen knew each other very well, and their ships were similar. Their techniques may have been borrowed from each other. Some of their ships going to Iceland may have been blown off course and accidentally come to America. Some of them might even have returned to the Mediterranean, and reports of a large body of land beyond the sea may have instigated a desire to send out a deliberate expedition to locate this land. "A large-scale migration to America . . . took place in three stages, beginning in 480 B.C.," Boland stated.

> Some of these migrants came to New England and stayed. Some strayed from the plotted course and came to the Chesapeake, whence they sailed north up the Susquehanna River, to settle in what is now Pennsylvania. Others strayed even more and sailed to the coast of South America.

Boland attempted to answer the question of why these people wanted to migrate in the first place. He proposed that one cause was the destructive Punic Wars, during which the Phoenicians were searching for new land to conquer. One of the cardinal needs in the Phoenician religion was for human sacrifice to accompany their rituals. This was suppressed by the new lords of Carthage and eventually also by the Romans when they took the Phoenician homeland. Boland said, "I think they came here for religious freedom. Human sacrifice, while not practiced with great frequency, was too fundamental a part of their religion to give up." He averred that the sacrificial stone at Mystery Hill, and a similar one at Leominster, Massachusetts, fifty miles away, did indeed exist for the purpose of offering human sacrifices, as the Phoenicians had done in their homeland.

Boland went on to describe Mystery Hill in detail, commenting:

Megalithic temples, it must be noted, are strewn all over the Middle East, as are menhirs and dolmens, both of which are in evidence. . . . I think we have a pattern. A pattern that traces a single culture. A culture that sprang from the Mediterranean and took root in England, Ireland, and the Americas.

However, Mystery Hill is by no means the only suspected Phoenician site in New England. Boland remarked, "In addition to the stone structures, there are two more mysterious signs that indicate the presence of Mediterranean people in New England."

He pointed to the carving of a Phoenician ship on a rock at Lake Assawompsett, Maine, that became visible when the waters of the lake receded. At the present time, the carving is again under water. It clearly shows a typical Phoenician ship.

I say it is Phoenician because it shows a yard at the top of the mast. Viking ships lowered their sails, yard and all, at anchor. The Phoenicians used a furling method similar to that used on later sailing ships: the sail was furled by being drawn up and fastened to the yard. When the ship was at rest, its silhouette presented a *T* shape, as opposed to a single stick of mast thrust up into the sky.

If it hadn't been for a drought in 1957, this carving would not have become known.

Another telltale sign mentioned by Boland is the rosettes and unfinished Doric column carved into the bedrock in Guildford, Connecticut. Hardly the work of American Indians!

If you wish to receive a copy of the latest BEAR & COMPANY catalogue and be placed on our mailing list, please send us this card.

Name _____ Date _____

(please print)

Address _____

City _____ State _____ Zip _____

Please check the following area(s) of interest to you:

1. ☐ Creation Spirituality   4. ☐ Healing/New Age
2. ☐ Medieval Mysticism   5. ☐ Native American/Mayan
3. ☐ Ecology/Sacred Sites   6. ☐ Other _____

BEAR & COMPANY
P.O. DRAWER 2860
SANTA FE, NM 87504-2860

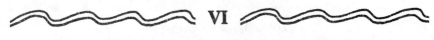

THE TRUTH ABOUT MYSTERY HILL

It is indeed difficult to arrive at the absolute truth about anything, and this applies to the archaeological site known as Mystery Hill. However, the interpretations I set forth in this chapter are not based on personal opinion alone, but on the materials and evidence at my disposal. Those who would disagree with me—and I'm sure there will be some—will still have to account somehow for the amazing parallels between Mystery Hill and other megalithic sites throughout the world.

First, I would like to examine the names, symbols, and characters provided by my three principal mediums. In analyzing the strange letters (or characters) drawn by Ingrid Beckman, I found a faint similarity with ancient European letters, but assigning these letters to specific alphabets was another matter. The first three characters drawn might be astrological symbols; reading from left to right, they would represent Jupiter or Zeus,

Figure 6. *Astrological symbols for Jupiter, Mars, and Venus.*

Mars or Aries, and Venus. Ingrid's remark that the third symbol represented a woman would reinforce this interpretation. I am sure that Ingrid was not aware of the proper astrological symbols for these three deities at the time she drew them.

The two characters in Ingrid's second line seem to tie in with the following two lines. They resemble early Cypriote script. What is com-

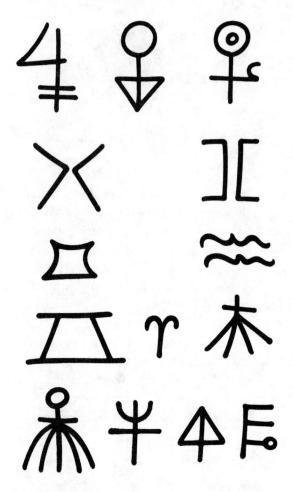

Figure 7. *Ingrid Beckman's psychic impressions.*

monly known as Minoan consists of symbols that are more in the nature of pictographs, although this is by no means the only Minoan script. The last line of characters was actually drawn by Ingrid prior to the other three lines, but it seems to tie in with the other characters, so it is thus rendered here for the sake of clarity. (Psychic impressions may not always come out in logical sequence.)

In comparing known Cypriote characters with the symbols drawn by Ingrid at Mystery Hill, it becomes apparent that, in Ingrid's four lower lines, nine out of eleven of her characters match the Cypriote characters

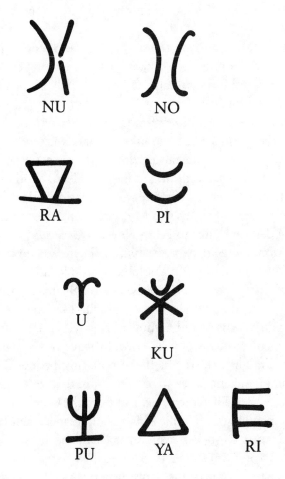

Figure 8. *Ingrid Beckman's samples of Cypriote script.*

pretty closely! (The Cypriote script reproduced here is based upon Barclay V. Head's *Historia Numorum*, published originally in 1914 and republished in 1963. Head was a curator at the British Museum.) Ingrid kept mentioning three gods—Titan, Pan, and Mesme—but she drew astrological symbols for the deities Jupiter, Mars, and Venus. It would seem that the intention was to express a parallel between the conventional names of these deities and the names used by her. There is little difficulty relating Titan to Zeus, since it was Zeus who, according to Greek legend, deposed the Titans, or more accurately Titanos, his father. Pan and Mars have sometimes been considered aspects of the same deity. However, when it comes to Mesme, or Mesma, as another form of Venus, I find myself stumped.

Ingrid later referred to another triad of deities: Sendar, Mesme, and Aron. She also mentioned Mesopotamia as somehow being involved in the background of those who came to Mystery Hill in an early era. Ethel Meyers also mentioned Mesopotamia.

There are these possibilities: Sendar may very well be a mispronunciation, or rather an inaccurate rendition, of Sandan. Sandan was a rather obscure deity who had significance primarily to the people of the Phoenician seaport of Tarsus. According to Barclay Head, Sandan was a local variety of Hercules. As for the name *Mesme*, the only deity with a name even remotely resembling this was Messene, sometimes called Messena, a secondary deity popular in Peloponnesian Greece.

As for Aron, there are two possibilities. There was, of course, Arion, a maritime deity whose ride on a dolphin astounded the Greeks as a near supernatural feat. There was also the city of Nisibis in Mesopotamia, whose local protecting deity was the constellation Ares. Seafaring people from various towns would naturally bring with them fond memories of their particular local deity and would want to worship their god wherever fate might lead them. If the seafaring people who came to Mystery Hill in ancient times were from more than one place, perhaps their gods were, too. Then there was also Ares, the Greek name for Mars.

There is mention of a Titanic Masma culture in ancient Peru, according to Dr. Daniel Ruso, an explorer specializing in South American cultures. Erich von Däniken refers to it also in *In Search of Ancient Gods*. It may well be that some of the South American archaeological puzzles tie in with Mystery Hill.

Behind the Sacrificial Table, there is a stone slab in an area described by Robert Stone as the "animal pen." On this stone, there is a carving of what appears to be a character resembling a pyramid with the top fifth cut off. Strangely enough, the identical symbol was drawn by Ingrid Beckman in her third line of characters. At the time Ingrid drew the character, she had not seen the stone with the identical shape carved on it. As of yet, I have not been able to match it with any known alphabet.

In dealing with inscriptions carved into stone, or petroglyphs, the first task is to examine the cutting surfaces to establish the probable age of the work. In addition, scrapings from the stone in the area where people

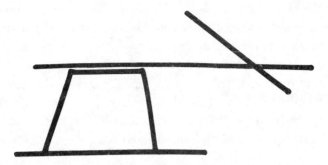

Figure 9. *Inscription in stone in back of Sacrificial Table. Drawing by Ingrid Beckman.*

have left their mark are examined via the radiocarbon dating process. Or, roots of trees that have grown into or through the rock in question are examined in the same manner. The stones mentioned throughout this book have already been thoroughly examined with respect to their age and the authenticity of their carvings. Nobody is being fooled by Native American markings or modern tourist graffiti. Those who are trained in archaeology, especially if they are also familiar with epigraphy and numismatics, can tell the difference between a recent inscription and an ancient one.

Some of the earlier accusations of fakery against unusual relics, such as the rune stones found in the heartland of America where there "shouldn't be any," were based on unusual choices of letters, antiquated forms, and other nonconformity with what the scholars of the day thought was the proper style. But long years of research with actual specimens have taught me that there is no such thing as a 100 percent norm.

Stones bearing inscriptions or drawings occur all over Mystery Hill. Undoubtedly, there were more at one time, but a portion of the stones were carried off by stone thieves, and a major earthquake occurred between the time these stones were inscribed and the present. This latter fact may account for the odd positioning of some of the larger stones. I have personally inspected a number of the inscribed stones at Mystery Hill and have found the inscriptions to be, beyond a shadow of a doubt, the result of human action upon natural stone, not figures due to temperature changes, natural growths, and other nonhuman causes.

One of the most remarkable stones at Mystery Hill is a boulder standing on the main site (see photo 30). As the photograph shows, it carries an inscription of several characters. The first character seems unusually large in relation to the following characters, but perhaps this was done on purpose. Having spent three years exploring the mysteries at this site, I do not venture to offer complete translations of the inscriptions. However, I am satisfied that the characters or letters on this boulder are indeed very early Greek and that they could not have been incised by any of the nationalities commonly associated with the site by traditional historians.

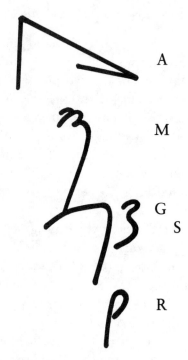

Figure 10. *Inscription in stone at main site.*

This particular boulder carries the letters *A M G S R*, reading from top to bottom. The style of each letter corresponds to what Edmund Maude Thompson, in his *Handbook of Greek and Latin Paleography*, calls Cadmean Greek, that is, very early Greek. In that time period, inscriptions were generally written from right to left. However, a top-to-bottom system was also used when space so dictated.

Another stone, standing west of the main site near the cliff where Indian pottery has been found in abundance, seems to correlate with the inscribed boulder just described (see photo 31). Although my first impression of it was that it carried several Punic or Phoenician letters, on closer examination I realized that this was not the case. The early Greek alphabet was directly derived from the Phoenician, and at that stage it was quite similar to its parent, but the inscription on the boulder near the Indian cliff is unquestionably early Greek. Moreover, it is a combination of a petroglyph, or rock drawing, and an inscription.

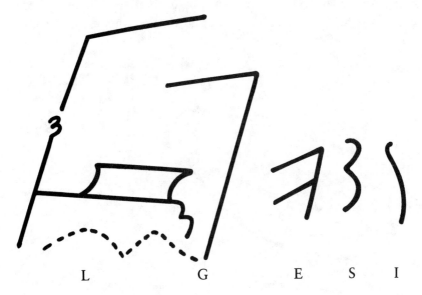

L   G   E   S   I

Figure 11. *Inscription in stone near cliff: Cadmean Greek, left to right.*

As the drawing shows, this stone portrays a simple but eloquent rendition of a ship surrounded by waves. Its prow is to the left, its large sail is in the center, and its rudder is to the right. Above it and to the right is an inscription that reads, from right to left, *I S E G L*. There may be an additional character beyond the *I* on the right, but I cannot make it out because weather has destroyed some of the rock's surface.

Assuming that *I S E G L* is the entire inscription, I can perhaps speculate on its meaning. *IS* means strength or power; *EG* may be an abbreviation for *egeiro*, which means "standing guard"; and the remaining letter, *L*, meant "eleven" in early Greek, although in later Greek it stood for the number thirty. Could the message be that eleven men stood guard here, having come by ship? This interpretation, of course, is only speculation. The inscription and rock drawings are facts.

At the main site there is another heavy boulder inscribed with what at first looks like strange letters. On close inspection, however, it becomes clear that these markings do not constitute an inscription at all, but a schematic drawing of a ship. Again, there is the main sail, the small sail in the rear (unless this is meant to be the rudder), and the prow in front. To the right of the ship is a somewhat smaller rendition of four columns, Grecian style, and a staircase leading up to them on the right. Were the people who carved this petroglyph trying to tell us they came by ship and built a temple on this site?

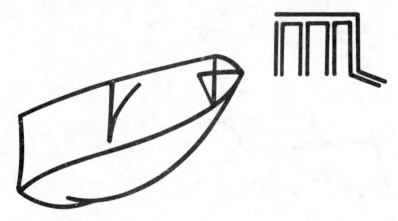

Figure 12. *Schematic engraving of a ship.*

In the administration building at Mystery Hill, there are several stones bearing inscriptions collected from around the site. One triangular-shaped stone has several lines of inscription that seem to differ from those found on the larger boulders (see photo 32). For one thing, the marks are much more shallow. Also, by comparison with European monuments, the arrangement and style of the letters suggest that they might be from a somewhat later period than those just discussed.

The characters on the larger boulders date from the second millennium B.C. at the earliest and the period just prior to 900 B.C. at the latest. These dates are based on characteristics of the letters, which I have carefully compared with known European examples. The triangular stone in the museum of the administration building, on the other hand, depicts Greek writing from the period between 900 and 500 B.C., in my judgment. In that period, inscriptions were read from left to right. The letters read *C H Y L E* in the first line. In the next line, the first letter may be *TH* or a drawing of a symbol; this followed by the letters *O M A U N*. Finally, there seems to be a partial third line in which I can make out for sure only the letter *R*. Such inscriptions are very likely to be legible only in part, and individual words were probably abbreviated, making proper reading very difficult indeed. It will take years of study to come to a final conclusion on what these inscriptions say, but that they are ancient Greek is certain.

CH Y L E

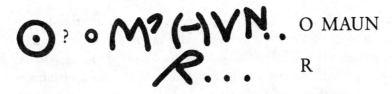

O MAUN

R

Figure 13. *Greek inscriptions on triangular stone: somewhat later Greek.*

Another of the stones on display in the museum is roughly five-sided in shape. It is lettered, as far as I can make out, in an early Greek alphabet. Again, the complete inscription cannot be read at this time, but it is possible to read, from right to left, the letters *A PH L N*. Below the inscription, there is a rough drawing of a ship, with the prow quite clearly visible. The only problematical aspect of this inscription is the second letter, *PH*, which, according to Thompson, occurs somewhat later in the development of the Greek alphabet. However, I propose that the letter might be a Greek kappa, in which case the problem would not arise. Or, perhaps, the use of the double sound *PH* was already acceptable at the time the inscription was made.

Another five-sided stone, measuring about twenty-two inches across,

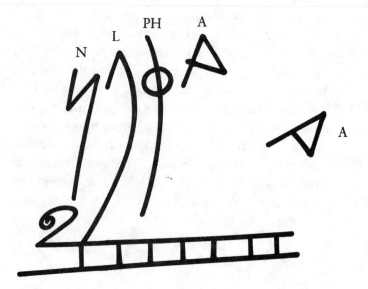

Figure 14. *Inscription in stone in museum showcase.*

bears a deeply incised inscription—or part of one, for the stone seems to be a piece of a larger stone that may be lost forever (see photo 33). The part that is legible bears characters that Thompson assigns to a slightly later period than the inscriptions found on the stone now housed in the museum showcase that I referred to previously. In this later period, inscriptions were written and read from left to right, rather than the archaic right to left. In concrete terms, this means that the stone was inscribed around 800 B.C., possibly 700 B.C., whereas the right-to-left inscriptions would be dated between 1200 and 900 B.C. There are five letters more or less clearly visible on this stone fragment. Reading from left to right, they are *E K N S I.*

Figure 15. *Inscription in stone from later period, 800-700 B.C.*

An ibex running to the left, carved onto a stone in the descending corridor wall of the Oracle Chamber, is one of the chief attractions at Mystery Hill and is always pointed out to visitors. Carvings of this kind are fairly common at prehistoric sites, beginning with Cro-Magnon caves, and they occur in Europe, Africa, and various parts of the New World. However, when considered in conjunction with the inscribed stones at Mystery Hill, the ibex takes on a somewhat different meaning. In view of the position of the stone inside the Oracle Chamber, which is connected with the Sacrificial Table, the drawing may be that of a sacrificial animal and not necessarily a domestic animal or hunt animal as it is in Cro-Magnon caves. All that is certain is that it is a drawing of a medium-sized running animal with horns, resembling a domestic or wild goat. The animal has been referred to as a running deer as well, although I cannot agree with that interpretation.

This covers the inscriptions discovered so far, which certainly represent only a small portion of the total inscribed stones of Mystery Hill. Many others lie beneath the soil or were carted away by stone robbers and are yet to be discovered in the future. All inscriptions seem to jell in terms of time and origin, except perhaps the characters clairvoyantly seen by Ingrid Beckman. Her characters were definitely Cypriote, although they were of the same period as the early Greek inscriptions found on the rocks. The Cypriote alphabet differed somewhat from the early Cadmean Greek alphabet, though it was also derived from the Phoenician. At the time in question, sailors from both Cyprus and Crete were active aboard Greek ships, and it may well be that nationals of both islands were among those who settled at Mystery Hill.

Mystery Hill has thus revealed elements of early Greek and Cypriote writing, and deities connected with not only the early, pre-Hellenic Greeks but also the so-called Phoenicians. I am saying "so-called" because most laymen and even some historians think of the Phoenicians as a Semitic people active primarily after 500 B.C.—the same people who helped found Carthage and there became known as the Punic nation. However, the Phoenicians, as used in this context by me, were the seafaring people from what later became known as Phoenicia—the country rather than the race. That they were Semitic is beyond doubt; but it appears that these pre-Phoenician Phoenicians actively worked with the pre-Hellenic Greeks. As they were better shipbuilders, they furnished the ships that they and the Greeks sailed to various parts of the world, known and unknown.

The drawings of ships found on the stones at Mystery Hill can be compared with the ships on existing monuments and coins of the later Phoenicians, and they are very similar in every detail. Charles Boland is sure that the Phoenicians (the early Phoenicians, that is) had contact with the early Norsemen, and that both nationalities benefited from each other's knowledge of shipbuilding. Thus, there were many similarities between Norse and Phoenician ships. Considering this, the mixture of nationalities that set foot on North American soil and came to Mystery Hill is in no way incompatible with the epigraphic evidence found. Nor is the evidence in any way contrary to the possibility of such people traveling beyond the Pillars of Hercules, eventually reaching New England, then continuing on the Merrimack River toward a landfall some distance inland, whence they would attempt to reach the highest hill in the vicinity—to wit, Mystery Hill.

In *Before Columbus*, Cyrus Gordon proposed that people from the Mediterranean area set foot on American soil centuries before Christ. These seafaring people included Phoenicians, Hebrews, and others throughout the Mediterranean area—even Romans at a later date. Gordon based this view on a theory called "Atlantic diffusion" by archaeologists—the idea that travelers from across the Atlantic Ocean brought samples of their civilization with them, established themselves in the New World, and left evidence behind in the form of artifacts. Gordon believed that diffusion took place for thousands upon thousands of years, not only across the Atlantic Ocean but across the Pacific Ocean as well. However, the majority of conventional archaeologists hold that parallel developments occurred in the Old World and the New World, and that these parallels account for similarities of cultures on both sides of the ocean.

As far as the United States is concerned, Gordon made an excellent case for landings by ancient Mediterranean people. He based his case not on similarities of cultures alone, but on solid physical evidence. There is, first of all, the stone dug up eighty years ago in the grave at Bat Creek, Tennessee. (This was mentioned in chapter 1.) The grave had never been disturbed previous to the find, as indicated by the roots of a dead tree that grew down through it and by the arrangement of the skeletal remains in the grave in two neat rows.

The stone itself was found and reported by archaeologists of excellent reputation. It contains five Hebrew letters and a numeral of a type similar to numerals on ancient Hebrew coins of the same period. Such coins were also discovered at three widely separated sites in Kentucky. The five letters on the Bat Creek stone read: "For the land of Judah, the year one."

At the time of its discovery, the inscription was thought to be Cherokee (!), and it was only later that its true nature was discovered. Anyone accusing the stone's discoverers of fakery must be reminded that the stone was discovered in the late 1880s, and a report on it was published in the annual report to the secretary of the Smithsonian Institution in 1890–1891. Native Americans would not have had the ability to copy down ancient Hebrew script, especially since it was not deciphered until the late nineteenth century and was not even analyzed properly until 1862. The Bat Creek grave is undoubtedly much older than the American Indian civilization in this area, which is something even the arch sceptics, hostile to the idea of a Hebrew relic in Tennessee, must admit. As Gordon put it in the *Science Digest* magazine article "Lost Cities and Forgotten Tribes,"

> I've thought through this, and there is no doubt about it, the only trouble with this stone, as another archaeologist said recently, is that it was discovered in the wrong place. If it had turned up in the Mediterranean, it would make a little footnote to some paper. But it's the spread of the Mediterranean culture to this continent that interests me. If this were found in Palestine, I wouldn't be interested in it.

Still another strong contender for evidence of the presence of Mediterranean people in the United States is the so-called Metcalf stone, found at Fort Benning by Manfred Metcalf, a civilian employee at the fort. In addition to exhibiting writing from the same Near Eastern area, it contains glyphs that are similar to Cretan symbols. All nine symbols on the Metcalf stone are identical to known Cretan symbols, according to Gordon.

Even more fascinating (or upsetting, depending on one's point of view) is the so-called Paraiba stone unearthed in Brazil in 1872. By January of 1874, New York scholars had exact transcripts of the stone's inscription. From then on, a controversy has raged concerning its authenticity for roughly the same reasons the Bat Creek and Metcalf stones are periodically attacked by people who simply can't accept the idea that they might just be genuine.

Cyrus Gordon has no doubts as to the authenticity of the Paraiba stone, which dates to the sixth century B.C. and contains an eight-line inscription in Phoenician script. The people who inscribed this stone in Brazil called themselves Canaanites. Gordon's translation of their inscription reads:

> We are the sons of Canaan from Sidon, from the city where a merchant prince has been made king. He dispatched us to this distant land, a land of mountains. We sacrificed a youth to the celestial gods and goddesses in the nineteenth year of Hiram, our king. *Abra!* We sailed from Ezion-Geber into the Red Sea and voyaged with ten ships. We were at sea together for around two years around Africa. Then we got separated by the hand of Baal and we were no longer with our companions. So we have come here, twelve men and three women, into one island, unpopulated because ten died. *Abra!* May the celestial gods and goddesses favor us!

The stone must have been carved around 530 B.C. Its presence in the wilderness of Brazil is an embarrassment, to say the least, to those who still do not believe that ancient people from the Mediterranean reached the New World.

One of the people I consulted immediately after I had completed my investigations at Mystery Hill was Frederick McLaurin Adams of Pasadena, California, probably one of the foremost experts on pagan religions and the archaeology relating to them. At the time, a team of three members of his own group, Feraferia, was in Colorado analyzing ground configurations along the Colorado River. These ley lines (magnetic meridians spanning the globe that the ancients considered especially important), related to those in England and elsewhere, are huge, and make sense only when viewed from the air.

I went to see Adams in California, bringing with me photographs of Mystery Hill. "The New Hampshire megalithic shrine sounds familiar to me," he said, after studying the evidence. "I have the feeling that your mediums' material is composed of ancient ecumenical hieroglyphs of the 'Peoples of the Sea,' contaminated perhaps with some elements of medieval cipher scripts. Mohenjo-Daroans, Samarians, Minoans, Mycenaeans, Hebrews, Egyptians, and Greeks were in the Americas from the fourth millennium—at the latest—onward. To say nothing of the influence of Atlantis, about which I no longer entertain any doubts." Adams then requested that when I went back East I send him a map and other material on Mystery Hill so that he could study it in depth. I did so, and a few weeks later he got in touch with me.

Fred Adams had been to Britain and the Mediterranean area only the year before, and the memory must have been fresh in his mind. "Mystery Hill is a henge [circle of stones] as well as a *hypogeum*, [underground chamber] as we find in Malta," he told me.

Professor Ross T. Christensen, of the Department of Anthropology and Archaeology at Brigham Young University, wrote in the January 1970 *Newsletter* and proceedings of the Society for Early Historic Archaeology: "The constructions were plainly not built by New England Indians or their ancestors of any known variety. They clearly do not fit into the pattern of prehistoric culture development usually assigned to the eastern woodlands area by professional archaeologists."

Christensen reported that the charcoal radiocarbon dating undertaken in 1969, which yielded the date of 1045 B.C., was one of the most important discoveries made at Mystery Hill. He warned against coming to any final conclusions until all the evidence was in, and in 1970 it was indeed not as plentiful as it is today. He evidently had no knowledge of, or paid no attention to, the inscribed stones at the site as additional and perhaps even more significant evidence for the dating of the site. Christensen pointed out that in Spain the Atlantic Bronze Age lasted as late as 700 B.C. He referred to similar constructions in Europe, especially in Spain and Portugal—significant parallels with Mystery Hill. But he was not prepared to identify the strangers from across the water by a known name. He stated:

> It looks as if the strange, rough-hewn structures of Mystery Hill and elsewhere in New England and New York State are about to be identified in terms of time periods and origin. And the evidence so far argues in favour of a trans-Atlantic crossing. But apparently those who came were not Indian hunters, Yankee farmers, Irish monks, nor Phoenician mariners; they were a nameless people of the late Bronze Age of the western Mediterranean area, perhaps from Portugal.

Joseph B. Mahan, Jr., of the Columbus, Georgia, Museum of Arts and Crafts, investigated the Yuchi Indians of Georgia and found certain connections between them and the people of the eastern Mediterranean. This brings up the interesting notion that some Indian tribes may contain elements of European ancestry, no matter how intermingled these are with later racial characteristics. It is conceivable that some Europeans who came to the Americas were not massacred by whatever local population existed but may have intermarried with Indians and produced a mixed race. There are strange traditions throughout Indian lore that suggest either foreign derivation or parallels beyond the law of chance. The odd language recorded phonetically by Ethel Johnson Meyers at Mystery Hill may be Indian, but I am more inclined to consider it an imperfect rendition of a Semitic tongue. The preponderance of hissing sounds, along with words like *yahimi* and *ishma* seem to indicate Near Eastern origin.

Professor Christensen later undertook a Mediterranean research project on the Phoenician civilization, both in the Old World and the New World. The outcome of his investigations was a paper entitled "The Phoenician Theory of New World Origins Re-examined," which was read at the Society for Early Historic Archaeology's seventeenth annual symposium on the archaeology of the scriptures in 1967. He continued his research in the Near East after that and read a second paper, "The Phoenician Theory of New World Origins," in 1968. As part of his investigation, he undertook a careful scrutiny of the Book of Mormon, in which there is mention of a Nephite-Mulekite civilization and a river called Sidon. This mention does not refer to the Atlantic seaboard but to inland America.

Christensen worked his way westward from Phoenicia itself, visiting Cyprus, Malta, Tunisia, Sardinia, Spain, and eventually the colonies founded by the Phoenicians beyond the Straits of Gibraltar on the Atlantic coast. It was clear to him that the people of Phoenicia were trying to extend their domain westward, and that this was a process of considerable duration. "Cyprus held what may have been the first overseas colonies of the Phoenician civilization," he remarked in the *Newsletter*. "One such was the kingdom of Kithion situated on the southeast coast facing Sidon and Tyre."

Perhaps the fact that Ingrid's symbols were of Cypriote origin may yet tie in with Phoenician domination, if the dates are correct. It is also possible that the characters I have tentatively identified as Cypriote may in fact be from a parallel alphabet of the same period, differing only in minor details. This would not be at all unusual with ancient Mediterranean alphabets, all of which had a common derivation.

"There has developed, largely among American scholars, a heightened curiosity about evidence favoring ancient trans-Atlantic crossings, particularly Phoenician ones," Christensen stated. "It may not be long until the whole subject of the origins of advanced civilization in ancient America by means of transoceanic diffusion from centers of Old World civilization can receive a fair, open-minded hearing on the part of the Americanist profession."

In Erich von Däniken's *In Search of Ancient Gods*, the author describes a number of inscriptions found on stone tablets in South America. A gold tablet depicting an Egyptian-type pyramid with letters at the foot of it is particularly interesting. The inscription seems early Phoenician, according to Edmund Maud Thompson in *Handbook of Greek and Latin Paleography*. The gold tablet was found at Cunca, Ecuador. According to Thompson, it carries fifty-six different letters or symbols. The Incas are known to have had no alphabet, so the script must have a much earlier origin. The inscription contains a number of easily recognized early Phoenician letters, so one can only wonder why establishment archaeologists have not yet fully investigated this find and published articles on it.

Ethel Johnson Meyers provided several words of an unknown language, phonetically spelled. The word *rit-me-i-a-tooi*, possibly pronounced "ritmiiatue," sounds, at least in the generic sense, like words given by H.E.L. Mellerish in *Minoan Crete*, to wit: *miami-ja-ra-ro, si-ja-pu-ro, pi-ja-se-me*. The words are from the excavations of Knossos, Crete. Among the symbols or drawings found on the tablets at Knossos are those of oxen, cows, sheep, goats, pigs, horses, and deer. They are just as schematically represented as the ibex found in the descending corridor of the Oracle Chamber at Mystery Hill. "The story of the evolution of writing in Crete is a complicated story, and the discovery of what use the Minoans mainly made of their writing is a somewhat surprising one, as well as disappointing," said Mellerish. "Equally complicated and even more surprising in its result, is the story of the efforts to decipher the scripts."

One of the most interesting relics found in Crete, the so-called Phaistos Disk, is a thick clay object, six and a half inches in diameter. It is covered on both sides with strange pictographs and has defied full explanation to this day. Even though the great archaeologist Sir Arthur Evans spent much time on it, in the end he never got any further than deciphering its Minoan numerals.

In *Mysteries from Forgotten Worlds*, Charles Berlitz displayed a photograph by J. Manson Valentine of a gold headpiece with grid writing. It is from the Crespi collection of Cunca, Ecuador. No attempt was made to decipher this grid, but it only takes a good look at the chart found in Thompson's book to see that several characters in this square are of early Greek origin. What they stand for is another matter. It may be that these letters were not put together into words but had symbolic meaning, were abbreviations, or were a code. However, the fact remains that very early Greek letters were inscribed on what appears to be an authentic gold relic from a very early age, unearthed in Ecuador, on the "wrong side" of the Atlantic.

Berlitz offered an interesting theory concerning the origin of the alphabet:

> Ancient seafarers would have needed an exact way of keeping count of days spent on voyages and may have designated and recorded numbers by simplified signs which also became an alphabet. It is known that, in the first alphabets, letters were used for counting as well as writing. . . . The mystery of the origin of the phonetic alphabet, therefore, may go back to an even older scientific attainment, that of counting, and the alphabet, if we follow the theory still further, may be the child of mathematics.

In the same work, Berlitz reproduced a remarkable tablet found at Glozel, near Vichy, France, in 1924. It has been the subject of much debate since, because, "although vouched for by many authorities of prehistory, [it] has been attacked as spurious, possibly because its acceptance as authentic would imply a sweeping re-evaluation of established theories," Berlitz said. The tablet was found among bricks, axes, and pottery of the Magdalenian era, and displays a number of letters, some of which are reminiscent of Phoenician and early Greek, while others are unidentifiable.

Again, I can only marvel at the lack of interest, if not blindness, of professional cryptographers and epigraphers with respect to this tablet, for several of the characters are clearly of early Greek origin. They resemble, not only in appearance but also in technique of incision, some of the stones found at Mystery Hill.

"Clearly defined writing of this era and in such a location is archaeologically unacceptable and, although the Glozel tablet has been vouched for by many prehistorians, the mystery still stands," said Charles Berltiz.

"A mystery which, if verified, would indicate that unknown people in northern Europe were able to write thousands of years before the Egyptians first developed their hieroglyphic script—a most unsettling concept to traditional archaeologists."

Berlitz also referred to another theory concerning prehistoric writing, published in 1971 by researcher Alexander Marshack and involving some finds in Aurignacian caves in France. "This would put written notation, if not writing, back about 30,000 years," Berlitz said.

When Ethel Johnson Meyers gave her phonetic rendition of the language she heard psychically at Mystery Hill, she stated that the people who had uttered the strange language lived there eighteen thousand years B.C. Perhaps these were not the same people identified by Ingrid Beckman—the early Greeks who flourished there between 1200 and 900 B.C. Quite clearly, there was a succession of races that came to Mystery Hill over very long periods of time and were perhaps separated from each other by stretches of time when the hill was uninhabited. This can only be guessed at through interpretation of the evidence.

If method of construction and similarity of stones mean anything, then there is a parallel to Mystery Hill in the Neolithic village of Skara Brae in the Orkney Islands, off the coast of Scotland. This excavated village was described in *The Monument Builders* by Robert Vernick and the editors of Time-Life Books. Thus far only ten stone houses have been excavated at Skara Brae; they are connected or separated by walls and linked by stone alleys. Vernick said:

> Apparently the people abandoned the town abruptly; this is suggested by a string of beads dropped in a passage and by partly ignored bones left by a bedside. It may be that Skara Brae's inhabitants fled from a storm as savage as the one that in modern times exposed their site anew.

That Mystery Hill was both a sanctuary/observatory and a settlement seems clear from what has been excavated thus far. The sanctuary/observatory occupied the highest part of the hill, while the houses in which people lived surrounded it, stretching out on all sides a considerable distance. Stonehenge was only an observatory, but it stood in the plains in the middle of well-known territory where villages might have existed safely at a distance from it. This arrangement was not so likely in America, where newly arrived seafarers would have tended to put their living quarters as close to the center of their religious and cultural identification as possible. Also, there was the probability of hostile natives in the surrounding area. The difference, then, between a Stonehenge and a Mystery Hill is the difference between a Gothic cathedral raised in the center of town and a fortified monastic complex incorporating both mundane and spiritual buildings.

Charles Michael Boland, though he placed the Phoenician migration to New England as late as 482 to 186 B.C., may have had the right reason for their arrival in the New World. He thought these travelers left the Phoenician world because their religious freedom was being interfered with when human sacrifice, an important cornerstone of their religion, was suppressed. He connected their flight to the New World with the destruction of Carthage by Rome.

However, every indication, from radiocarbon dating and inscribed stones to psychic readings, points to a much earlier age. The Phoenicians who arrived at Mystery Hill had nothing to do with the classical Phoenicians who inhabited the same homeland at a later date. These were the ancestors of the Semitic peoples who resided in what is now Lebanon in 500 B.C., and their need to find new land may indeed have been due to difficulties at home, although perhaps not due to the political-religious difficulties Boland envisioned.

In the sixteenth century B.C., a great natural catastrophe befell the island of Thera, or Santorini. Most of the island blew up, causing atmospheric changes for years to come. Between 1400 and 1200 B.C., nearby Crete suffered disastrous earthquakes and fires that leveled nearly everything at Knossos and elsewhere on the large island. It was to this same time, 1200 B.C., that my psychics dated the arrival at Mystery Hill of strangers from the Mediterranean. Could it be that the seafaring people from the eastern Mediterranean, whom I have called the "pre-Phoenician Phoenicians," came to America because their homeland was in a state of disarray due to natural catastrophes and the aftermath of economic blight, disease, and political anarchy?

Historical records show that Crete and other islands of the Aegean were never quite the same after the catastrophes. It took them a long time to rebuild, and, even then, what emerged was a different way of life. I think that those who left the Aegean, including not only Semitic but also

Greek people, wanted no part of the reduced and uncertain life that the post-catastrophe world represented. They deliberately set out to conquer new worlds beyond the Pillars of Hercules and eventually wound up at Mystery Hill.

Since this would imply not simply a handful of people but a considerable wave of immigrants, it is certain that not all of them went to the same place. All over the Western Hemisphere, there is evidence of Greek and Semitic landings. I have already mentioned the various Phoenician and other ancient inscriptions on stones found in widely separated areas of the United States, even far inland, such as in Tennessee and Kentucky. However, traces of Phoenician colonies have also been found in Mexico.

James Bailey said in *The God-Kings and the Titans*:

> Competition from the western sea-peoples and the Mycenaeans in the Mediterranean was one influence to stunt the growth of mainland Phoenicia. But once the Mycenaean Greeks and the Peoples of the Sea had destroyed each other, the Phoenicians again flourished, as the Arabs were to do later under somewhat comparable circumstances. The first European dark age was that period between 1200 and 700 B.C. when Phoenician civilization flowered.

As evidence of widespread Phoenician travel, Bailey pointed to the Paraiba stone, which I mentioned previously as an indication of Phoenician presence in South America, and to a second inscription found on a stone near Rio de Janeiro, three thousand feet up on a vertical wall of rocks. Translated, the inscription on the second stone reads, "Tyre, Phoenicia, Badezir, first born of Jethbaal . . . " The stone has been dated to the middle of the ninth century B.C.

Bailey made an interesting point concerning the development of this early Phoenician sea power.

> Following the collapse of Pelasgian and Mycenaean sea power, Phoenicia had prospered, with her hands firmly on what used to be Pelasgian and Greek trade. Settlements of Phoenician merchants were already to be found in Egypt during the reign of Amenophis II (1440 to 1414 B.C.).

Carthaginian, that is, Phoenician, colonies existed on the west coast of Africa. As late as the fourth century A.D., there was a report by the Bishop of Hippo that the Phoenician language was still spoken on the

African west coast. On the island of Corvo, the westernmost island of the Azores group, a terra cotta horseman was discovered by the Portuguese. It was pointing westward, in the direction of America. Corvo is only a thousand miles from Newfoundland. Punic, that is, Carthaginian colonies have been discovered as far as twenty-six hundred miles from Gibraltar; thus, a distance of a thousand miles would have created no great barrier to the seafaring Phoenicians.

Bailey painted a persuasive picture of Phoenician influence in Mexico based upon stone artifacts, manner of building and construction, and religious practices. He listed parallel after parallel, supported not by guesswork but by physical, archaeological evidence. At La Venta, on the gulf coast of Mexico, where the heart of the Olmec culture dated to about 800 B.C., the evidence is particularly overwhelming.

> Of the great altars found at La Venta, altar number one bears the North Syrian pattern of a twisted rope, which we have already found elsewhere in Mexico. The impressive feature of this altar is the seated figure underneath it, which resembles a curious ceramic piece now at the Louvre, found in Cyprus, and believed to have been consecrated to the Phoenician goddess Astarte. Altar number two carries the figure of a man, carved in the round, apparently sacrificing unwilling children. The third altar was made out of one of the great stone heads of the African type, flattened on top, and with a speaking tube going in at the ear and out at the mouth for working oracles, very much after the style of the oracles known from Babylon.

Bailey commented that a comparison between Aztec glyphs of Mexican origin and Cretan characters found on the Phaistos Disk shows not similarity but identity of at least eight symbols, proving that one was derived from the other. He also noted that at the town of Balsas, on the Balsas River in Mexico, a small clay figurine was unearthed in 1928 that was practically identical with figures of Melkarth, the idol of Carthage and Phoenician Tyre. The celebrated headdress of feathers worn by King Montezuma was very similar to the feathers worn by the Minoan kings. Even linguistically, many words of ancient Mexico were similar to Phoenician and early Greek words. It is inescapable that Mexico received this knowledge and civilization from the Old World.

However, the Phoenicians were by no means the first European people to arrive on Mexican shores. There are many parallels between the language and customs of the Aztec predecessors, who spoke Nahuatl, and early European languages and customs. Bailey said, "These were essentially symbols of Mediterranean people of the second and third and fourth millennia B.C., starting seemingly with Aryans, certain Semites, and Samaritans."

The Maya of Guatemala also showed strong links with the Old World. Among the deities worshiped by the Maya was Xaman-Ek, associated with merchants and writing and also known as the North Star God. Bailey said, "The Phoenicians were so famous for sailing at night by the North Star, that in the Old World the North Star was at one time called The Phoenician." Ethel Johnson Meyers, while ruminating amongst the ruins at Mystery Hill, spoke of a planet called Yahitma Hooh, a planet belonging to Polaris, the North Star. Immediately after this, she mentioned Phoenicia. What the connection might be—if any—is unclear, but it bears noting.

The parallels between the Phoenicians and the Maya are many and impressive. Cylinder seals, generally associated with Mesopotamia and later Phoenicia, have been found in Mayan territory in large numbers. The similarities between the Phoenician, early Greek, and Mayan alphabets are astounding, to say the least: *A* is called aleph in Phoenician, alpha in Greek, and ahau in Mayan; *G* is gimel, gamma, and ghanan; *L* is lamed, lambda, and lamat; and so forth. Bailey commented:

> In many cases, the Phoenicians and the Maya have very similar "characters" for the same letters and also similar meanings for the characters. Now the Maya cannot possibly have hit upon not only the names, but also the order as in the Phoenician alphabet. So at first sight it looks as if the Mayan script had come from the Phoenicians. But the Phoenician characters are very simple, in contrast to the complicated day-symbols of the Maya. It therefore seems probable that both scripts have a common root, older than the Phoenician script, from which they both developed.

Bailey argued that this old script consisted of hieroglyphs, that is, it was pictorial. He felt that the origin could hardly have been Egypt, for Egyptian hieroglyphs were based on totally different principles. However, he found them

> extremely like the symbols of the ancient Cretan script. Both scripts have simple symbols like circle, cross, hand, eye, etc.; but both also contain many symbols so abstract you cannot see what picture they

were taken from. . . . We may therefore safely say that the Mayan legends were right: Kukulcan, their White God, taught his people the script he brought with him. And this script was Cretan.

As mentioned before, the east coast of America was by no means the only place where the enterprising Mediterranean seafarers landed and founded colonies. Evidence of European Bronze Age colonists in Peru is visible and convincing. Bailey said, "Behind Peru and Bolivia were the creative energy of the Semitic sea-people, the Aryans and the Sumerians, their astronomical, mathematical, and navigational skills, their knowledge of irrigation farming, their proclivity for terraced agriculture."

The Incan term for Peru means "Land of the Four Quarters," while the official title for the king of Akkad, Mesopotamia, was "Ruler of the Four Quarters." Tapestries found at Pachacemak, Peru, show ancient symbols practically identical with Old World scripts of the Bronze Age. Bailey noted:

> The Aztec name for temples was *teocallis*, for their ancient city of priests was Teotihuacan; for this centre of culture in Peru, ruled by priest-kings, the name was Tiahuanaco. The Mycenaean word for god is *teo* and in Greek Cretan Linear B, *wanak* means king.

One hundred and fifty miles north of the city of Cuzco, Peru, a stone tablet bearing twenty-two incised characters was found. A similar tablet was also found in Bolivia. Bailey offered no translation for the strange inscription. In my opinion, he reproduced it upside down in his book. When I turned the inscription the other way around, it made a lot more sense to me. Whether it is read from left to right or from right to left is difficult to say. However, the inscription contains several early Greek *A*'s, a kappa, and several lambdas. With some effort, it could probably be deciphered. This would be a long and tedious job that might take years and a number of qualified researchers. What they should keep in mind is that letters and symbols used by the ancients weren't always formed exactly as they were supposed to be. Local variation, a whim of the moment, an inability to write properly, and other such factors might very well have altered a letter or symbol considerably.

E.J.W. Barber said in *Archaeological Decipherment*:

> Inscriptions from diverse sites and periods may also vary considerably in form. If the sign types are very hard to match, particularly if there

is any evidence that the inscriptions from the various sites or eras may represent different languages (as may well be the case with some of the inscriptions tagged as Linear A), it is far wiser to limit the corpus right at the start to the largest single body of homogenous inscriptions.

As I went about trying to piece things together, other elements made more and more sense, even though they had not done so at the beginning. For instance, Ingrid Beckman and Ethel Meyers both mentioned Ethiopia, which I thought was outlandish in the context of our investigations at Mystery Hill. Later, I discovered that according to Bailey, "the Phoenicians are said by Herodotus to have migrated from the Erythrean Sea, which comprised the Red Sea, the Persian Gulf, and the Arabian Sea, to the Levant." In other words, from Ethiopia to the Near East. Ethel Meyers, without even having set foot on the site, kept speaking of "red men" all around her. This, of course, led me to believe she was talking about Indians. Again, Bailey provided a significant statement: "The name *Phoenician* was given to them by the Greeks; it means 'Red Men' and was also applied by the Greeks to the Minoan Cretans."

Bailey suggested that the designation *Phoenician* had to do with paint the Phoenicians put upon themselves or, more likely, because they were famous for trading in purple cloth, a most desirable item in antiquity. The Phoenicians referred to themselves as Canaanites. According to Bailey:

> The name *Phoenician* is sometimes used widely for the people of Byblos, Ugarit, Minoan Crete, Tyre, Sidon, and Carthage; sometimes it is prescribed more narrowly for the *historical* Phoenicians after 1200 B.C., the cities of Tyre and Sidon, and their colonies. I use the wider denotation in this essay, as did the Greeks themselves.

About 3000 B.C., a great change took place on the island of Crete. The Neolithic and rather primitive population was gradually replaced by a people using metal for their tools and arms. This was the beginning of the great Minoan civilization, which provided fine arts utilizing gold and precious stones. With it came an advanced technology. The Cretans themselves, according to Bailey, seemed to have come mainly from Syria and were of Semitic origin. This indicates a blending of Semitic peoples and civilizations from the Near East that gradually became "Greek" in terms of geography and culture.

Thus, it is clear that true distinctions cannot be made among Greeks, Minoan Cretans, Phoenicians, and Semitic peoples in general. In the early stages of development, they were all one. Even the Cypriote characters psychically described by Ingrid Beckman fit into this pattern of an emerging multinational civilization, for Cyprus was also part of this group of states—the emerging Bronze Age civilization that preceded classical Greece by many centuries.

Inscriptions similar not only to some at Mystery Hill but more importantly to Phoenician inscriptions from Europe and Asia have been discovered on rocks in Brazil. An inscription from Manaos is a nearly exact duplicate of one found in Sidon, dated to around 500 B.C. Another one, also from Manaos, matches an early Phoenician inscription known to David Diringer (*The Alphabet*).

I have already mentioned that symbols found on the Metcalf stone in Georgia match symbols of Linear A and B Greek exactly, according to Cyrus Gordon. Again, this connection is far more than a vague parallel or coincidence. Gordon thought that the text on the stone might be some kind of inventory. Moreover, the Yuchi Indians, on whose land the stone was discovered, have a strong tradition that they originally came to America "from the East."

Bailey's *The God-Kings and the Titans* is an excellent study of the many, often intricate, parallels and similarities between ancient concepts and those found among the people of the Americas. It is important to realize Mystery Hill does not represent a unique situation, even though in terms of position and magnitude it may well deserve the title of "America's Stonehenge." Unusual discoveries continue to be made.

Donald Ness, while trucking water to fight a forest fire at Hawley, in northeastern Pennsylvania, discovered an unusual stone inscribed with characters of a totally unrecognizable type. Although they had a faint resemblance to runes, they were not found to be runic upon examination. According to Dr. Vernon Leslie in the *Canadian Journal of Anthropology*, "Competent scholars to whose attention the rock has been called have so far failed to relate the inscription to any known script." It never occurred to them, apparently, to look in a good dictionary of archaic Chinese characters, for that is what they seem to be. That the ancient Chinese came to America is not exactly unknown. According to Charles Michael Boland, "A Chinese . . . sailed across the Pacific to bring the message of Buddhism to the barbaric peoples of this land. He arrived in A.D. 499." His name was Hoei-Shin. The characters found on the Pennsylvania stone fit this time period.

Petroglyphs, or inscriptions incised on rock, have been found all over the Western Hemisphere. At Lake of the Woods, Ontario, Canada, the Phoenician letter *N* was found on a stone. At Red Lake, also in Ontario, Canada, another stone with the Phoenician letter *G* was discovered. A *D* showed up on a rock at Dighton, Massachusetts. A very clear *F* (digamma) of early Greek origin graces a stone at Horwood Lake, Ontario, Canada. Cliff Lake, Ontario, Canada, has a somewhat later Greek *N*, from perhaps a century or two after the early Greek inscriptions at Mystery Hill.

In 1968, the New England Antiquities Research Association acquired the collection of inscribed and grooved stones found in the 1940s by the late Dr. W.W. Strong of Mechanicsburg, Pennsylvania. They may have come from a stone structure on top of Stone Mountain, which was one of the sites where the association wanted to dig. Helped considerably by Cyrus Gordon, the New England archaeologists were able to establish that some stones, at least, bore Phoenician letters. The characters for *T*, *G*, *B*, and *V* appear quite plainly on some of the stones.

"It is Dr. Gordon's opinion . . . that the inscribed stones from Dr. Strong's collection represent an actual script. Whether it is indeed Phoenician, or somehow derived from it, is one of the questions we hope to find a definite answer to," reported Robert Stone in the September 1968 NEARA *Newsletter*.

According to this issue of the *Newsletter*, a strange artifact came to light ten years prior at Cripple Creek, Colorado. An antique dealer, R.J. Wills of Monroe, Louisiana, acquired it as an "Indian artifact." Since it didn't look like one, he contacted Jack McGee of Fort Worth, Texas, who had done work on the Heavener rune stone. The stone had a six-line inscription carved into it, which McGee mistakenly identified as fourth-century Gothic until, with the help of Professor Vincent Cassidy of the University of Southwestern Louisiana, he discovered that the writing was Greek.

The inscription translates as "Here lies the servant of God, Palladeis." However, it is ambiguous and could also be read as "Here I sacrifice the slave of the god Palladeis" or "I, Palladeis, slew the slave of the god." Whatever the translation, the inscription is clearly pre-Christian Greek, although the age of the characters indicates a later period than the material at Mystery Hill. However, if the inscription relates to a pagan sacrifice, it may well be that it dates back to the very end of the Mediterranean occupation of that area. The form of the letter *eta* used precludes this inscription being any more recent than around 800 B.C.; it may be older.

In an article entitled "A Lost City on the Susquehanna?" freelance journalist Ellen Chappelle spoke of an exciting find of inscribed stones at the junction of the Susquehanna River and the Conodoguinet Creek. The article appeared in the spring 1967 NEARA *Newsletter* and included drawings of some of the stones found at the site. One of them clearly portrayed a charging bull, while another carried what appeared to be a three-character inscription.

I have not seen the actual stones and can rely only on the rendition of the inscriptions in drawings, so I cannot be sure of the interpretations of the letters. However, on first reading they also seem to be early Greek. I can make out an *A* followed by a *G* on one stone. Another stone from the same group quite clearly shows an early Greek letter *M* as well as what appears to be an extensive inscription. Much of it, however, has become obliterated. In addition to the charging bull, other animals also appear on these carved stones. Mrs. Pietsch, who found the stones, points out that the area where she picked them up is like an island, as it is located at the junction of the two rivers. She feels that if Phoenicians were involved in the carvings, they would have built their cities on islands that could be easily defended, as they did in their homeland in Europe. Chappelle quotes Mrs. Pietsch as saying:

> The washed rocks from subsequent trips revealed an entire menagerie: bears, a beaver, a cow, a ram, rabbits, and some indeterminate objects. . . . For this reason, I think they may be tangible relics of an ancient settlement. If its founders were Phoenicians, they, being a mercantile people rather than plunderous, possibly selected this site for an outpost, as it was centrally located in respect to navigation. . . . Hence, these animal carvings might be in some ways advertisements of their wares; or appeals to the gods for good hunting; or even cult objects for worship of the animals themselves. . . . This settlement may also have had its marking stones. Large boulders, ten by fifteen approximately, set in the river bed and covered with inscriptions and pictographs, could have been a notice to voyagers that they were almost there. Until recently, about six or seven of such stones were readily visible, and at present one can still be seen at low water, directly below the Safe Harbor Dam. Another was removed to the museum at Harrisburg; and the remaining ones (about five to ten miles south of the dam) are permanently flooded over.

In the March 1971 NEARA *Newsletter*, Leon N. Morrell, Jr., stated that, as of that date, in addition to the Mechanicsburg Phoenician alphabet stones, similar carved stones had been reported at the following locations:

> Safe Harbor, Pennsylvania; Mystery Hill, New Hampshire; Raymond, New Hampshire; Mount Number Seventy, Tennessee; Phoenician inscription of New Mexico now in custody of Brigham Young University; the Paraiba inscription, Brazil; stones found at Mount Jessie, Alton, New Hampshire; stones bearing Phoenician inscriptions found in the Amazon Valley, Brazil, in the first half of this century; stones bearing Phoenician-like inscriptions found in Virginia in 1950.

In the spring 1974 *Newsletter*, Sarah Johansen published an article on the discovery of a fertility figure at a New England site. She did not disclose the location of the site in order to protect it from the curious. Photographs that accompanied the article showed a stone slab crudely engraved with a fertility image similar to those found in the Old World.

In an article entitled "Possible Phoenician Cultural Parallels at Mystery Hill," by Gertrude B. Johnson (March 1962 NEARA *Newsletter*), parallels were drawn between Phoenician-Carthaginian building methods and cult habits and the material found at Mystery Hill. In particular, Johnson compared the so-called Tanit Precinct of Carthage (sacred to the Moon Goddess, who was also the Goddess of Death) with certain carvings at Mystery Hill.

> The square stelae of the Tanit Precinct, with their deeply carved architectural facades centering on a sacred symbol, have an affinity to a strangely contoured stone on the southern end of the cliff section of Mystery Hill. . . . Nearby, in the woods near the cliff, are large stones with hollowed-out depressions that could have been seats.

In the fall of 1967, NEARA archaeologist James Whittall discovered buried in the earth near a ruined chamber an inscribed stone slab that was roughly triangular and measured about fourteen by seventeen inches. The piece was much worn and seemed to have been underground for a long period. However, some of the incisions on it were still quite deep and indicated tool marks. Whittall remarked in the *Newsletter*:

> NEARA member Marjorie Kling has examined the markings on this rock and feels that they bear far more similarity to inscriptions from the eastern Mediterranean than to any Amerindian petroglyphs. Further interesting possibilities showed up when the stone was pho-

tographed with a strong side lighting. We saw what appeared to be the head of a large deer-like animal with a smaller one beside it, both full-faced; also a schematized running deer or ibex, and the head of a similar animal without horns or antlers, shown in profile. Recalling the "running deer" (or ibex) carving and that, under certain lighting conditions, a bull's head shows on one of the orthostats at the Tomb of Lost Souls in another part of the site, these apparent features may be more than accidental and have real significance.

In June 1968, we found another stone in the Megaron area of the site, which could well be an ancient sun symbol; the centre dot seems to have been made deeper at some later date.

These findings represent incontrovertible evidence of ancient presences in the United States of America. Inscriptions, building methods, artifacts, and, finally, radiocarbon dating, support the notion that ancient mariners from the Mediterranean came to the United States and settled. When I speak of "early Greek," I am speaking of the people to whom the Phoenicians also belonged, since it has been established, following Cyrus Gordon's lead, that Cretan civilization was derived from the Semitic Phoenician world. Thus, the Minoan Cretans coming to America belonged to the same wave of immigrants as the Phoenicians. Their migration perhaps stretched over a considerable period of time, which allows for certain differences in their script. Ingrid Beckman said that she felt the period of their presence was between 1200 and 700 B.C. It was during this period that writing changed in one important respect: characters began to be read from left to right rather than from right to left.

The presence of people from the eastern Mediterranean began even before the second millennium B.C. and ended early in the first millennium B.C., perhaps as late as 700 B.C.; this much has been accounted for. What has not been accounted for is the presence of celestial visitors amongst these immigrants, hinted at by all three mediums I brought to the site. Since the mediums had no way of discussing their tasks with one another, and since I had not informed them of any of my own thoughts or given them an opportunity to hear about theories from others, each of their readings is prima facie evidence, unconnected from the others. This ties in with Erich von Däniken's theory of "visitors from space": humanoids regarded as gods by the terrestrial races receiving them.

Whether these superior visitors came directly from space or whether they were Atlanteans who, in turn, had come from space at an earlier period of time is a moot question. This book is not about the validity of

Atlantis and Lemuria, but deals with the origins of Mystery Hill and, peripherally, with other such unusual sites in North America. My feeling is that superior beings did indeed come to America from time to time, perhaps, as was suggested, to help the natives with their problems or to prevent human sacrifice, which had been brought to American shores by the Mediterranean arrivals—one can only guess. However, it should be recalled that Mystery Hill, in antiquity, was not as wooded as it is now, and it stood out prominently in the surrounding countryside as the highest point within a very large area. Whether seen from the sea or from the air, Mystery Hill was a place that would evoke the curiosity of any stranger.

In summary, what Robert Stone has dubbed as Mystery Hill is a very ancient site, prominent in the surrounding countryside, which was populated at first by primitive people of little cultural understanding. Later, an invasion, whether by design or accident, of people from the eastern Mediterranean arrived there and created a settlement around a central observatory/sanctuary. Still later, perhaps when the settlement began to decline in its morality, visitors from a higher civilization appeared to deal with the settlers. Ultimately, some Norsemen and Irish Culdee monks may also have been there, although there are no artifacts to support this, as least as far as the exact site is concerned. As time went on, Native Americans came to live in the area, followed by colonial settlers and modern people.

Fortunately, some establishment scientists are slowly coming around to the idea that ancient people did indeed settle in America. In the middle 1980s, Professor Barry Fell of Harvard, one of America's top experts in ancient writings, said in a television interview concerning Mystery Hill, "There is absolutely no doubt about it. I found three inscriptions at the temple. They were in Celtic, a European language. And by comparing them to other Celtic inscriptions found in Portugal, I was able to date them back to between 900 and 600 B.C."

He was able to translate one of the inscriptions at Mystery Hill as "Dedicated to the Sun God, Bel." Another inscribed stone, found at the same site, he read as "Embellished by . . . cut this stone." (This interview was conducted by me for a television documentary entitled "In Search of Strange Visitors," which I wrote and produced.)

Fell, who is the author of *America B.C.*, pointed out also that Mystery Hill shows strong similarities to England's Stonehenge. Four giant stone slabs are strategically placed exactly where the sun rises and sets on the longest and shortest days of the year—June 21 and December 21. Fell stated he was "convinced that we now have sufficient evidence to show that an advanced culture existed in America as far back as three thousand years ago. But as to how it got here, that is still a mystery."

When he spoke of Celtic people, Fell was not referring to today's Celts (the Irish, Scottish, and Welsh), but rather the Ibero-Celts who originally came from the eastern Mediterranean—in other words, people from Greek areas such as Minoan Crete and pre-Semitic Phoenicia. The Celtic sun god, Bel, of whom Fell spoke, was really none other than the Phoenician Bal, counterpart to the Hellenic Phoebus Apollo.

What stands out about Mystery Hill is its true origin and the manner in which American archaeologists have avoided accepting the evidence for it. The idea that ancient biblical people settled in America is indeed so overwhelming that some may prefer not to know about it. However, the stones have spoken, and those who wish to see for themselves need only visit Mystery Hill.

Pompeii went under in A.D. 70 but was not rediscovered until the 1700s—a few odd items found on the grounds of a site often do not encourage a massive search for more. Undoubtedly, other as yet undiscovered sites and artifacts await the curious. However, it is as difficult to overcome an established dogma about the discovery of America, such as the one involving Columbus, the Norsemen, and Saint Brendan, as it is to overcome the religious dogma of a church. People are frightened by new things that may replace cherished notions with which they have become comfortable. Doctors tend to ignore new, unorthodox findings for as long as possible, under the guise of needing more evidence, instead of digging in and trying them out. Accepting new findings means learning new things, and, more importantly, unlearning old things.

It is deplorable that NEARA has only limited funds to proceed with its admirable work of discovering further artifacts and buildings on and off the site of Mystery Hill. Only a massive excavation of the entire area can yield additional clues—the kind of clues that would establish the site as the number one archaeological site in North America. Despite occasional publicity in the written media and on television, nothing has happened on an official level to support the work of the association.

Let this book spark some enterprising explorer with the right knowledge and outlook to go after what is truly America's forgotten past.

SELECTED BIBLIOGRAPHY

Ashe, Geoffrey. *Land to the West*. New York: Viking Press, 1962.

———. *The Quest for America*. London: Pall Mall Press, 1971.

Bailey, James. *The God-Kings and the Titans*. New York: St. Martin's Press, 1973.

Barber, E.J.W. *Archaeological Decipherment*. Princeton: Princeton University Press, 1974.

Berlitz, Charles. *Mysteries from Forgotten Worlds*. Garden City, NJ: Doubleday, 1972.

Boland, Charles M. *They All Discovered America*. Garden City, NJ: Doubleday, 1961.

Brennan, Louis A. *American Dawn*. London: Collier-MacMillan, 1971.

Daniel, Glynn. *Megaliths in History*. Levittown, NY: Trans-Atlantic Arts, 1973.

Diringer, David. *History of the Alphabet*. New York: Newbury Books, 1983.

Edwards, Frank. *Strange World*. New York: Ace Books, 1964.

Fell, Barry. *America B.C.* New York: New York Times Books, 1978.

Furneaux, Rupert. *The World's Most Intriguing Mysteries*. New York: Ace Books, 1966.

Gilbert, Edgar. *History of Salem, New Hampshire*. Salem, NH: privately published, 1907.

Goodwin, William B. *The Ruins of Great Ireland in New England*. Boston: Meador Publishing (now Forum Publishing), 1946.

Gordon, Cyrus. *Before Columbus*. New York: Crown Publishing, 1971.

Hapgood, Charles H. *Maps of the Ancient Sea Kings: Evidence of Advanced Civilization in the Ice Age*. Philadelphia: Chilton Books, 1966.

Hawkins, Gerald S. *Beyond Stonehenge*. New York: Harper and Row, 1973.

Holden, Raymond. *The Merrimack. Rivers of America* Series. New York: Rinehart, 1958.

Keel, John A. *Our Haunted Planet*. Greenwich, CT: Fawcett, 1971.

———. *Strange Creatures from Time and Space*. Greenwich, CT: Fawcett, 1971.

Lovecraft, H.P., and August Derleth. *The Dark Brotherhood*. Sauk City, WI: Arkham House, 1966.

McKern, Sharon. *Exploring the Unknown*. New York: Praeger Publishing, 1972.

Mellersh, H.E.L. *Minoan Crete*. New York: G.P. Putnam's Sons, 1967.

Olson, Tryggvi J. *Early Voyages and Northern Approaches, 1000-1632*. New York: Oxford University Press, 1964.

Perry, Clay. *Underground New England*. Brattleboro, VT: Stephen Daye Press, 1939.

Pohl, Frederick J. *The Lost Discovery: Uncovering the Track of the Vikings in America*. New York: W.W. Norton, 1952.

Renfrew, Colin. *Before Civilization*. Cambridge, MA: Cambridge University Presss, 1979.

Seton, Anya. *Avalon*. Boston: Houghton Mifflin, 1965.

Sloane, Howard N., and Russell H. Gurnee. *Visiting American Caves*. New York: Crown Publishing, 1966.

Steiger, Brad. *Atlantis Rising*. New York: Dell Publishing, 1973.

Taft, Lewis A. *Profiles of Old New England*. New York: Dodd, Mead, 1965.

Thomas, Bill. *Tripping in America*. Philadelphia: Chilton Books, 1974.

Thompson, Edmund M. *Handbook of Greek and Latin Paleography*. New York: D. Appleton and Company, 1893.

Trento, Salvatore Michael. *The Search for Lost America*. Chicago: Contemporary Books, 1978.

Vernick, Robert. *The Monument Builders*. New York: Time-Life Books, 1970.

Von Wuthenau, Alexander. *Unexpected Faces in Ancient America*. New York: Crown Publishing, 1975.

ABOUT THE AUTHOR

Prof. Hans Holzer, Ph.D., is the author of ninety-six books, including *Window to the Past, ESP and You, The Alchemist, Life Beyond Life, The Ufonauts, Great American Ghost Stories,* and *Star in the East.* He has also written extensively for magazines and newspapers and has been a producer and writer of television documentaries, notably "In Search of . . . " (NBC). He lectures extensively.

Dr. Holzer studied at Vienna University in Austria and Columbia University in New York. He received his Ph.D. in philosophy from the London College of Applied Science. He taught parapsychology for eight years at the New York Institute of Technology and is a member of the Authors' Guild, Writers' Guild, New York Academy of Science, and the Archaeological Institute of America. He is listed in *Who's Who in America* and makes his home in New York.

MAP 2.

Astronomical alignments
at Mystery Hill

EXTREME POINTS OF THUBAN
1750 B.C.

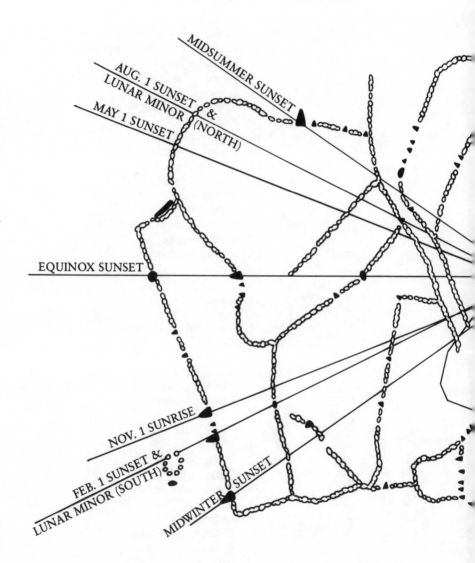

MIDSUMMER SUNSET

AUG. 1 SUNSET
LUNAR MINOR
& (NORTH)
MAY 1 SUNSET

EQUINOX SUNSET

NOV. 1 SUNRISE

FEB. 1 SUNSET &
LUNAR MINOR (SOUTH)

MIDWINTER SUNSET

MAP 1.

*Main site, Mystery Hill,
North Salem, New Hampshire*

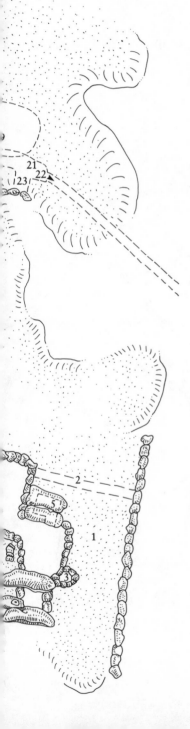

LEGEND

1. Pattee area
2. Sump pit
3. Upper well (Well of the Crystals)
4. Carved circle/tool-sharpening groove
5. Chamber/root cellar
6. Pattee cellar hole
7. L-shaped wall
8. Stone steps/"Megaron area"
9. Roof slab
10. Pattee's fireplace
11. Chamber in ruins
12. 2000 B.C. excavations
13. Entrance vestibule
14. Upper drain
15. Secret bed
16. Speaking tube
17. Roof opening
18. Oracle Chamber
19. Bedrock "seat"
20. Sacrificial table
21. Running ibex carving
22. Lower drain
23. Exit (created by vandals)
24. "Closet"
25. Exit to ramp drain
26. Ramp drain
27. 173 B.C. radiocarbon specimen
28. East-west chamber
29. The "V" hut
30. Compound
31. Mensal stone
32. Drain exit
33. "The pulpit"
34. Quarry post socket
35. 90° drilled hole
36. Large chamber
37. Undetermined structure
38. Drilled ledge
39. Large wall
40. Sundeck chamber
41. Pathway to Oracle Chamber
42. 2000 B.C. excavations
43. Triangular stone

NORTH

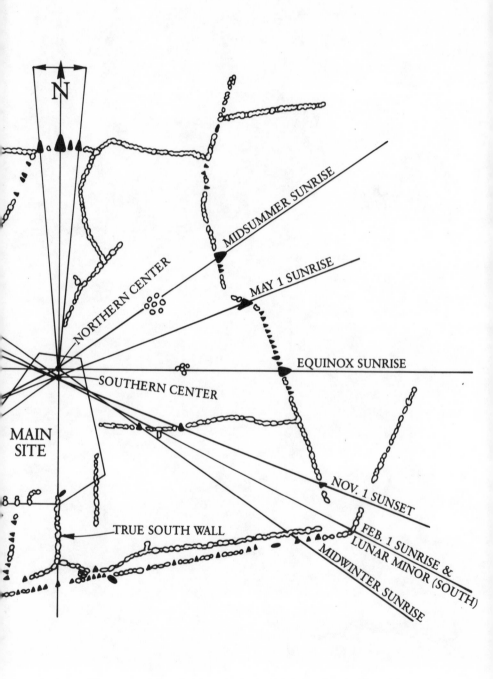

N

MIDSUMMER SUNRISE

MAY 1 SUNRISE

NORTHERN CENTER

EQUINOX SUNRISE

SOUTHERN CENTER

MAIN
SITE

NOV. 1 SUNSET

TRUE SOUTH WALL

FEB. 1 SUNRISE &
LUNAR MINOR (SOUTH)

MIDWINTER SUNRISE